e.guides

Ancient Rome

LONDON, NEW YORK, MELBOURNE,
MUNICH, and DELHI

Project Editor Jane Chapman

Weblink Editors Niki Foreman, John Bennett, Clare Lister

Senior Editor Claire Nottage

Managing Editor Linda Esposito

DTP Coordinator Siu Chan

Jacket Copywriter Adam Powley

Jacket Editor Mariza O'Keeffe

Jacket Designer Neal Cobourne

Publishing Managers Andrew Macintyre, Caroline Buckingham

Project Art Editor Ralph Pitchford

Senior Art Editor Jim Green

Managing Art Editor Diane Thistlethwaite

Consultant Dr. Philip de Souza, University College Dublin

Picture Research Debra Weatherley

Production Emma Hughes

Produced for DK by Toucan Books Ltd.

Managing Director Ellen Dupont

First American Edition, 2007

Published in the United States by DK Publishing, Inc.,
375 Hudson Street, New York, New York 10014

07 08 09 10 11 12 9 8 7 6 5 4 3 2 1

Published in Great Britain by Dorling Kindersley Limited.

A catalog record for this book is available from the Library of Congress.

ISBN-13: 978-0-75661-955-8
ISBN-10: 0-7566-1955-6

Color reproduction by Colourscan, Singapore
Printed in China by Toppan Printing Co. (Shenzen) Ltd.

Discover more at
www.dk.com

e.guides

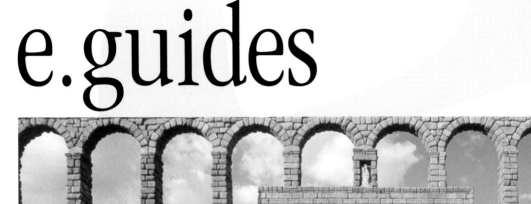

Ancient Rome

Written by **Peter Chrisp**

CONTENTS

How to use the e.guides Web site

e.guides Ancient Rome has its own Web site, created by DK and Google™.
When you look up a subject in the book, the article gives you key facts and
displays a keyword that links you to extra information online. Just follow
these easy steps.

http://www.ancientrome.dke-guides.com

1 Enter this Web site address...

Address : @ http://www.ancientrome.dke-guides.com

2 Find the keyword in the book...

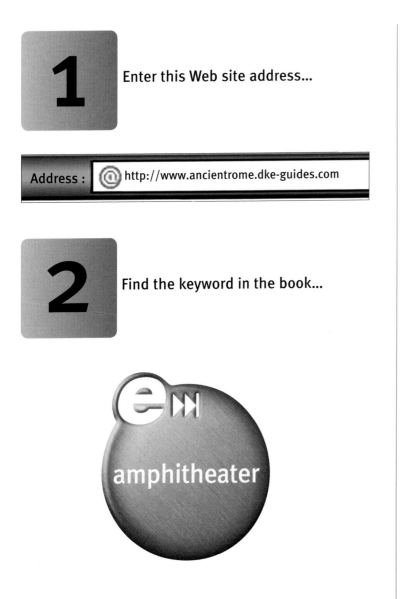

3 Enter the keyword...

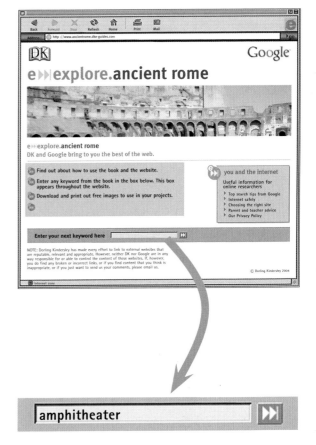

amphitheater

You can use only the keywords from the book to search
on our Web site for the specially selected DK/Google links.

Be safe while you are online:

- Always get permission from an adult before connecting to the internet.

- Never give out personal information about yourself.

- Never arrange to meet someone you have talked to online.

- If a site asks you to log in with your name or email address, ask permission from an adult first.

- Do not reply to emails from strangers—tell an adult.

Parents: Dorling Kindersley actively and regularly reviews and updates the links. However, content may change. Dorling Kindersley is not responsible for any site but its own. We recommend that children are supervised while online, that they do not use Chat Rooms, and that filtering software is used to block unsuitable material.

4 Click on your chosen link...

▶▶ Discover more about gladiators

Links include animations, videos, sound buttons, virtual tours, interactive quizzes, databases, timelines, and realtime reports.

5 Download fantastic pictures...

Pictures | Ancient Rome ▶▶

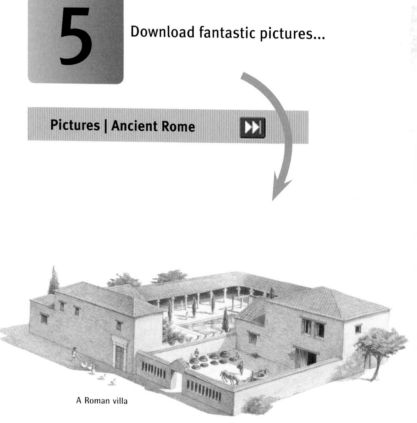

A Roman villa

The pictures are free of charge, but can be used for personal, non-commercial use only.

Go back to the book for your next subject...

THE ROMANS

Some 2,000 years ago, the Romans created one of the biggest and best-organized empires the world has ever seen. Throughout their lands, they built towns and roads, and spread their way of life. In far corners of the empire, people dressed in Roman clothes, used the same coins, and worshipped Roman gods.

One of the reasons why their empire was so successful was that, unlike other ancient states, the empire welcomed outsiders. Foreigners could become Roman citizens. At first this was given as a reward for loyalty or for service in the Roman army, but under Emperor Caracalla, who ruled 211–217 C.E., citizenship was granted to every free inhabitant of the empire. From the north of Britain to Egypt's Nile River, everyone apart from slaves could now call themselves "Romans."

York
BRITAIN
London
Dover
Gesoriacum
GAUL
Pyrenees
Nimes
SPAIN
New Carthage
MAURETANIA   NUMIDIA

◄ BECOMING A ROMAN
Many Roman emperors were not from Rome itself, but were from other parts of the empire, such as Spain, Africa, and the Balkans. This bust shows the emperor Septimius Severus, who ruled from 193–211 C.E. Severus was an African, born in Lepcis Magna in what is now Libya. His wife, Julia Domna, was a Syrian. The Severan dynasty he founded governed Rome for more than 40 years. The bust, which combines two different types of stone, shows the wonderful skill of Roman sculptors.

◄ LUXURIOUS LIVING
The Roman empire won loyalty by offering a higher standard of living to the upper classes. In Britain, where even the richest people had previously lived in simple, thatched round houses, Roman rule brought unimaginable luxuries. The rich could now drink wine, eat from beautiful tableware, and decorate their homes with mosaics (pictures made from small tiles). Even the less well off could afford to visit a Roman bathhouse, with rooms warmed by underfloor heating. This mosaic shows a drinking party by the Nile River.

▲ THE CONQUERED
While the rich benefited from Roman rule, life was much harder for those at the bottom of society. Poor peasant farmers had to work just as hard as they always had done, but they now also had to pay tax to the Roman government. This mosaic, from Algeria, shows two chained prisoners of war, their faces filled with despair. Such prisoners, captured in Rome's wars, would be sold as slaves and forced to work in mines or on great farming estates. The Romans could not imagine life without their slaves.

Romans

Baltic Sea

GERMANY

Elbe

Rhine

Danube

DACIA

BOSPORAN KINGDOM

Caspian Sea

Alps

Cremona

Ravenna

Po

Adriatic Sea

ITALY

Black Sea

ARMENIA

Falerii

Veii

Asculum

THRACE

Corsica

Rome

Cannae

MACEDONIA

Byzantium

Capua

Beneventum

Nicaea

GALATIA

Sardinia

Pompeii

Paestum

Tarentum

Heraclea

Brundisium

Pharsalus

Pergamum

Euphrates

Tigris

Tyrrhenian Sea

Actium

Thermopylae

ASIA

Messina

GREECE

Athens

Ephesus

SYRIA

MESOPOTAMIA

Enna

Ionian Sea

Corinth

Delos

Emesa

Babylon

Carthage

Sicily

Syracuse

Rhodes

Mediterranean Sea

Cyprus

Crete

JUDAEA

Jerusalem

Dead Sea

AFRICA

Lepcis Magna

Masada

Cyrene

Alexandria

ARABIA

CYRENAICA

EGYPT

Antinoopolis

Nile

Red Sea

▲ THE EMPIRE AT ITS HEIGHT

This map shows the Roman Empire in 117 C.E., when it stretched for 2,300 miles (3,700 km) from north to south, and 2,500 miles (4,000 km) from east to west. For the only time in history, all the lands around the Mediterranean Sea, which the Romans called *Mare Nostrum* ("Our Sea"), formed a single state. Roman rule provided peace and stability, helping trade, agriculture, and industry.

ROMAN ARCHEOLOGY

ANCIENT CITY
In lands once ruled by the Romans, there are hundreds of fascinating sites for archeologists to study. This circular building is a market hall in Lepcis Magna, in Africa. After being sacked by North African Berber tribes, in 523 C.E., the city was abandoned to the desert. Excavations didn't begin until the 1920s.

SEABED
The Mediterranean seabed is scattered with pottery containers, called *amphorae*, which were once used to store wine, olive oil, and various foodstuffs. These are often all that survive from Roman shipwrecks. By studying *amphorae*, archeologists can build up a picture of ancient trade routes.

GOLD MINE
Archeologists also study Roman industrial sites, such as ironworks and gold, silver, tin, and lead mines. This stark landscape, in Las Medulas in northwestern Spain, was created by Roman miners, who hollowed out a whole mountain to extract the gold. This was one of the biggest goldmining areas in the empire.

WRITING
This relief from Viminacium, in what is now Serbia, shows a banker holding a notebook. Surviving Roman writings include letters and other documents, preserved in the sand of Egypt or the wet soil of northern Britain. We can still read hundreds of Roman books, which have been copied and recopied for centuries.

BEGINNINGS

The Romans claimed that their city had been founded in 753 B.C.E. by Romulus, son of Mars, the god of war. After ruling for 40 years as Rome's first king, Romulus was believed to have been carried away into the sky, where he became a god. Romans were so proud of their city that they were sure that the gods must have had a hand in its birth. In fact, archeologists have shown that Rome was founded much earlier, growing from a humble group of small huts on the Palatine, one of the city's seven hills.

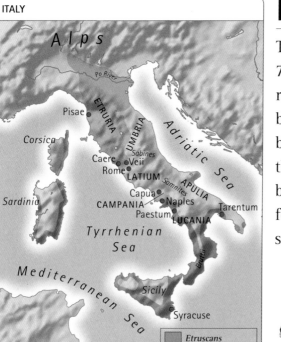

ITALY

In the 1st millennium B.C.E., Italy was home to many peoples, speaking around 20 different languages. The Romans were just one of the Latin-speaking peoples living on the west of central Italy, on the plain known as Latium. Rome was on the northern boundary of Latium, where it met Etruria—the land of the people known as Etruscans. A tribe called the Sabines lived in the hills to the northeast of Rome. To the south were the Samnites, and cities founded by Greeks. Settlers from Carthage, in North Africa, had also founded cities in Sicily.

Etruscans
Carthaginians
Greeks

◄ FIRST ROMAN HOUSES
In the 9th century B.C.E., the first Romans cremated their dead and buried the ashes in small models of huts made of pottery or bronze. Such urns may have served as houses for the dead in the afterlife. This bronze vessel shows us what an early Roman house would have looked like. On the Palatine Hill, archeologists have found postholes cut into the rock for huts just like this. The wooden posts supported walls of wattle (interwoven twigs) covered with daub (mud, clay, and straw), and thatched roofs.

ETRUSCANS ►
The greatest influence on the early development of Rome came from the Etruscans, whose civilization dominated northern Italy. They lived in a dozen or so rich states, each centered on a city and ruled by a king. Etruscans were wonderful artists, who created beautiful wall paintings and bronze and terra-cotta (fired clay) statues. The Etruscans were greatly influenced by the Greeks of southern Italy. This wall painting shows an Etruscan playing an *aulos*, a pair of pipes from ancient Greece.

ETRUSCAN INFLUENCE ON ROME

ART
An Etruscan artist, called Vulca of Veii, made the terra-cotta statue of Jupiter in Rome's most important temple on the Capitoline hill. This Greek-style statue of the god Apollo from the 6th century B.C.E., was found in Veii, north of Rome, and may have been made by Vulca himself.

TELLING THE FUTURE
Etruscans examined the livers of sacrificed animals to tell the future, a practice known as haruspication. A clue to their methods is provided by this bronze model of a liver, linking different parts of the organ with areas of the sky, each home to a different god.

TOGA
Etruscans wore a long robe called a *toga*, and leading noblemen had a *toga* with a purple border. Both were adopted by the Romans. This bronze statue of an Etruscan, called Aulus Metellus, dates from the 1st century B.C.E., when Etruria had become part of Rome's empire.

FASCES
Important Roman public officials, called magistrates, were accompanied by attendants, called lictors, who carried *fasces* (bundles) of rods with an axe in the middle. The *fasces*, another Etruscan invention, represented the magistrate's power to beat and execute offenders.

SHE-WOLF ►

One of the oldest surviving works of Roman art, dating from around 500 B.C.E., is this bronze she-wolf, which was probably made by an Etruscan artist living in Rome. The she-wolf played a central role in the legend of Rome's beginnings. Romulus and his twin brother Remus, grandsons of King Numitor of Alba Longa (in Latium), were abandoned as babies on the orders of their great-uncle, Amulius, who had seized Numitor's throne. They were found by a she-wolf, who looked after them as her own. At the foot of the Palatine Hill, there was a sacred cave where she was thought to have reared the twins.

Twins added in the 16th century

beginnings

THE FIRST SEWER ►
It was not until the late 7th century B.C.E. that Rome began to look like a town. To drain the marshy land at the foot of the Palatine, the Romans widened a stream running into the Tiber River, and gave it stone sides. The reclaimed land was then paved, forming a public square called the Forum. This picture shows the stone-lined stream, later called the *cloaca maxima* (great sewer), where it flows into the Tiber.

▲ SABINES
Early Rome attracted a mixed population, including Etruscans and Sabines, as well as Latins. According to legend, the Sabines were in Rome because Romulus and his men had seized Sabine women during a religious festival in order to populate the newly founded city. This painting by Jacques-Louis David shows the women, years after their capture, halting a battle between their Roman husbands and the Sabine men who had come to rescue them.

GREEK INFLUENCE ►
There were many Greek cities in southern Italy and Sicily, including Poseidonia (Paestum), which was named after the Greek sea god, Poseidon. This temple, originally dedicated to Hera, wife of Zeus, was built in Poseidonia around 450 B.C.E. The Romans were greatly influenced by Greek art, architecture, and religious ideas. They came to believe that many of their own gods were the same as the Greek gods, even though they had different names.

▲ CONSULS
This coin shows one of Rome's two consuls accompanied by lictors (attendants). To prevent any one man from becoming too powerful, a consul served only for a year, and he could not be reelected again for ten years. The main role of consuls was to command the armies, and to propose new laws. The two consuls had to work together, because each had the power to veto (reject) the other's proposals.

THE REPUBLIC

Until the late 6th century B.C.E., Rome was ruled by kings. The last king of Rome was an Etruscan, called Tarquin the Proud. He offended Rome's nobles, so they drove him out. Then, in around 510 B.C.E., they set up a new form of government, called a Republic ("affair of the people"). Rome was now governed by annually elected magistrates, the most important being two consuls who were heads of state. The consuls ruled with the advice of the Senate, an assembly of around 300 serving and ex-magistrates. Every adult male citizen had the right to vote for the magistrates. Since a magistrate's work was unpaid, only the richest could afford to stand for election.

THE SENATE ▶
In this relief, Roman senators walk in a religious procession. In theory, their role was to give advice to the 34 to 36 serving magistrates. The Senate had the advantage of being a permanent body, however, and, consisting of former magistrates, it had vast experience in government. Over time, the Senate's advice took on the binding force of law. Foreign policy and legal, religious, and financial issues were all decided by the Senate. Although laws were also passed by assemblies of the people, where the citizens could vote, these had first been proposed by the Senate.

RELIEF ON THE ARA PACIS ALTAR, IN ROME

TIBERIUS AND GAIUS GRACCHUS

◀ TRIBUNES
In the 5th century B.C.E., citizens of common birth (plebeians) won the right to elect their own officers, called tribunes. There were ten tribunes, whose role was to protect ordinary people from unjust acts by magistrates, and to propose laws to be passed by the people's assemblies. In practice, however, tribunes came from the same wealthy families as the senators, and they usually put the interests of the Senate first. It was only in the late 2nd century B.C.E. that two tribunes—the brothers Tiberius and Gaius Gracchus—used their powers to challenge the rich. They tried, but failed, to distribute land to the poor. Tiberius Gracchus was murdered by a mob of senators and their supporters in 133 B.C.E. His brother killed himself in 121 B.C.E..

the Republic

◄ DICTATOR
In emergencies, a dictator, who had unlimited powers, could be appointed for a limited period and special purpose. In 458 B.C.E., a consul and his army were besieged by the Aequi, a people from the hills east of Latium. The Senate decided that a man named Cincinnatus, who owned a small farm, should be appointed dictator. Messengers from the city found him plowing his fields. Within 16 days, Cincinnatus had gathered an army, defeated the Aequi, resigned his office, and returned to his plow (seen here with victory wreaths on the handle). His modest behavior has been used as an example of old-fashioned virtue throughout history. This was a man who did not let power go to his head.

NEW MAN ►
For 300 years, all but 15 of Rome's consuls came from a small number of noble families, who saw the office as their birthright. They called themselves *nobiles* ("known men"), the origin of our word "noble." Consuls whose families had not held high office before were known as "new men," and were looked down on by the nobles. One new man was Gaius Marius, who was consul seven times between 107 and 86 B.C.E. As consul he conquered Numidia in Africa and saved Rome from invasion by two huge Germanic tribes. Yet in spite of his successes, the *nobiles* felt superior to Marius. Unlike them, he had no busts of famous ancestors in his house.

GAIUS MARIUS

THE PATH OF HONOR

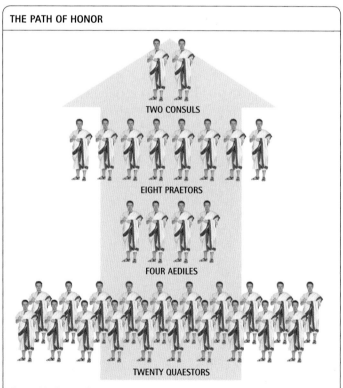

TWO CONSULS

EIGHT PRAETORS

FOUR AEDILES

TWENTY QUAESTORS

For wealthy Romans living in the 1st century B.C.E., there was a set career route called the *cursus honorum* ("path of honor"), leading to a position in one of the magistracies (shown above). At 18, they would join the army, usually serving ten years in the cavalry. They might then work in the courts, because skill in public speaking and understanding of law was needed for a political career. At 30, they stood for their first magistracy, as one of the 20 *quaestors* responsible for Rome's finances. Then they could serve as one of four *aediles*. These were magistrates in charge of public works, policing Rome, and organizing public shows. At 39, they might be elected as *praetors*, the eight senior law officers who oversaw the courts. Finally, at 43, they could become consuls.

INSIDE THE CURIA ►
This is the Curia, or Senate House, where the senators sat in rows along each side. Sessions of the Senate lasted from dawn to dusk. Each member gave his opinion from his seat, with the older ex-consuls speaking first. After the debate, a vote was taken, and the decision reached was recorded as the *senatus consultum* ("advice of the Senate").

ROME AND ITALY

From the earliest years of the Republic, the Romans fought to defend themselves against their neighbors and to extend their territory. The Romans were tough fighters, but they were also politically astute, making military alliances with other cities in order to bring them under Roman control. Gradually, the Romans either made allies of, or conquered, first the settlements of Latium south of Rome, and then the more distant Italian peoples. Through alliance or conquest, Rome eventually came to dominate the whole of Italy, providing vast reserves of manpower for future wars.

WARRIORS ▶

These are Lucanian warriors—members of a people from southern Italy—depicted on a wall painting in Paestum, the Greek city in southern Italy that they captured in 410 B.C.E. The earliest Roman soldiers were armed like these men, with round shields and long, thrusting spears. At some point between the 4th and 2nd centuries B.C.E. they adopted long, oval shields, which offered better protection, and javelins. One of the secrets of Roman success was their willingness to try new methods of fighting.

Blocks of tufa, a volcanic stone

SACRED GEESE FROM THE TEMPLE OF JUNO, ON ROME'S CAPITOLINE HILL

◀ GAULS SACK ROME

In 390 B.C.E., Rome suffered a disastrous setback when Gauls captured and sacked the city. According to legend, the only part of the city not taken was the Capitoline Hill, which was saved when sacred temple geese raised the alarm. The Gauls were bought off with a vast amount of gold. When the Romans complained to the Gallic leader Brennus that the weights used to measure the gold were too heavy, he threw his sword onto the scale, saying "Woe to the conquered!"

◀ NEW WALLS

Following the Gallic attack, the Romans determined that they would never allow their city to be captured again. In about 378 B.C.E., they built new fortification walls around their city. These were 7 miles (11 km) long and enclosed the city's seven hills. Later Romans called these the Servian Walls, in the mistaken belief that they were built by an early king, Servius Tullius. Protected by these new walls, which were 15 ft (4.5 m) thick and at least 28 ft (8.5 m) high, Rome would not be sacked again for 900 years.

Roman leads
two oxen

BRONZE OF A SAMNITE
WARRIOR

Bronze
breastplate

Hand once held
a spear

Rome and
Italy

◄ SAMNITE WARS

The most difficult wars
that Rome had to fight were those
against the warlike Samnites, whose
homeland was in the Apennines,
the mountain chain running down
the center of Italy. There were three
Samnite wars—in 343–41 B.C.E.,
327-304 B.C.E., and 298-90 B.C.E.—
each ending in Roman victory. By
the end, Rome controlled all of
northern and central Italy.

PYRRHIC VICTORIES ►

In 281 B.C.E., Rome quarreled
with the Greeks of Tarentum,
in southern Italy. They
appealed for help from
King Pyrrhus of Epirus, in
northwestern Greece, who
invaded Italy with an army
of almost 30,000 men and
20 elephants. Although he
defeated the Romans in two
battles, he suffered disastrous
losses. Congratulated on his
second victory, he declared, "One
more victory like that and I shall
be ruined." This is the origin of the
term "Pyrrhic victory," one gained
at too heavy a price. In 275 B.C.E.,
Pyrrhus returned to Greece
with less than one-third
of his original army.

▲ ROME'S COLONIES

In order to extend Rome's power, new cities, called colonies, were
founded in conquered territory. This relief shows a ceremony in which
a new colony's boundaries are being marked out by two oxen pulling a
plow. Romulus, Rome's founder, was said to have marked out the first
boundaries of Rome this way. Colonies were also established in existing
cities, such as Antium (present-day Anzio) in central Italy, which was taken
from the Volsci in 338 B.C.E. The colony served as a military stronghold, and
also helped spread the Latin language and Roman way of life.

ROMAN HUMILIATION

In 321 B.C.E., during the Second Samnite War, a Roman army led by two consuls
surrendered to the Samnites after being trapped in a narrow pass. This was a
humiliating defeat for the Romans, because the soldiers had not even fought.
In this picture, the Romans, stripped of their armor and weapons, are made to
walk beneath a yoke—the wooden crosspiece that attaches animals to a plow—as
a symbol of total submission. The captured consuls signed a peace treaty, which
the Senate refused to accept. The Romans always hated admitting defeat.

PYRRHUS DEFEATS THE ROMANS AT
THE BATTLE OF HERACLEA, 280 BC

THE PUNIC WARS

Rome's rise to power in Italy led to conflict with the rival empire of Carthage, a city in North Africa that controlled western Sicily, Sardinia, Corsica, and southern Spain. Between 264 and 146 B.C.E., the Romans fought three wars against Carthage, during which time Rome built up its navy to become a great seafaring power. These wars are called Punic after *Punicus*—the Latin name for the Phoenicians, the Middle Eastern people who were the original settlers of Carthage.

Roman warships, powered by oarsmen, with soldiers on the decks

▲ WAR AT SEA

The First Punic War broke out in 264 B.C.E., when the people of eastern Sicily appealed to Rome for help against the Carthaginians. In order to beat the Carthaginians, the Romans had to learn how to fight at sea. Luckily, they managed to get hold of a wrecked Carthaginian ship, and built 100 copies of it in just 60 days. Although two fleets were lost in storms, the Romans replaced them. In 241 B.C.E., the war was won and Sicily became Rome's first overseas province.

HANNIBAL ▲

Hannibal Barca (c.248–c.183 B.C.E.) was the son of Hamilcar Barca, the leading Carthaginian commander in the First Punic War. Hamilcar brought up his son to share his own loathing for Rome and he made him swear an oath of undying hatred for the city. It was an oath that Hannibal never forgot, because he dedicated his whole life to Rome's destruction.

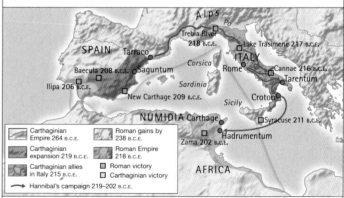

CARTHAGINIAN EMPIRE

Carthaginian Empire 264 B.C.E.	Roman gains by 238 B.C.E.
Carthaginian expansion 219 B.C.E.	Roman Empire 218 B.C.E.
Carthaginian allies in Italy 215 B.C.E.	□ Roman victory
→ Hannibal's campaign 219–202 B.C.E.	□ Carthaginian victory

This map shows the Carthaginian and the Roman empires, and the major battles in their struggle to be the leading power in the western Mediterranean. Following the First Punic War, in which Carthage lost Sicily, the Romans seized Corsica and Sardinia. The Carthaginians responded by extending their foothold in Spain to create a new empire.

◄ CROSSING THE ALPS

After becoming commander in Spain, Hannibal launched a new war with Rome. His daring plan was to lead an army out of Spain and launch a surprise attack on Italy from the north. The Second Punic War began in 218 B.C.E., when Hannibal set off at the head of 90,000 infantry, 12,000 cavalry, and 37 elephants. It took him 15 days to cross the snow-covered Alps, the high mountain range between Italy and Gaul. During the perilous crossing, he lost many men and most of his elephants.

THE BATTLE OF CANNAE

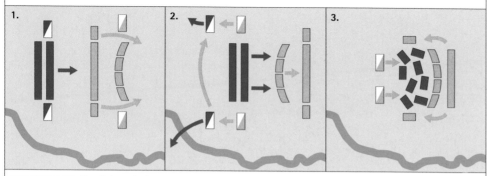

Romans
☐ Infantry
◪ Cavalry
Carthaginians
☐ Infantry
☐ Cavalry

Hannibal was the best general the Romans ever faced, winning battle after battle against them. His greatest victory came at Cannae, in 216 B.C.E., where he destroyed an entire Roman army of 80,000 men. (1.) After meeting the strong Roman center, Hannibal slowly pulled back his frontline, making the enemy think that he was retreating. (2.) The Romans kept pushing forward, walking straight into a trap. For while Hannibal was withdrawing his center, he sent his best troops to attack the advancing Romans on their exposed flanks. (3.) The trap was then closed by Hannibal's cavalry, attacking the Romans from behind. Rome learned a valuable lesson from this defeat. Force alone was not enough; they would need brilliant military commanders as well.

PUBLIUS CORNELIUS SCIPIO

AFTER CANNAE ▶
Following Cannae, almost all of southern Italy switched sides from Rome to Carthage. Yet, although Hannibal continued to campaign in Italy for another 13 years, he could never defeat the Romans entirely. He did not have a large enough army to besiege Rome itself, and the Romans never gave up. They continually raised more armies to replace those destroyed by Hannibal. This Carthaginian breastplate is just the sort of armor that would have been worn by Hannibal.

SCIPIO AFRICANUS ▶
In 210 B.C.E., the young Publius Cornelius Scipio was made Roman commander in Spain, where he defeated Hannibal's brother, Hasdrubal Barca, in battle. Appointed consul in 205 B.C.E., Scipio took the war to Africa, defeating Hasdrubal a second time. Hannibal was now recalled from Italy to defend Carthage. In 202 B.C.E., he faced Scipio in battle near Zama. In the words of the Roman istorian Livy, "the two most famous generals and the two mightiest armies of the two wealthiest nations in the world advanced to battle". The victory went to Scipio, who was honored with the name, "Africanus" (Scipio of Africa) for winning the Second Punic War.

Punic wars

RUINED ROMAN BATHHOUSE IN CARTHAGE

◀ CARTHAGE DESTROYED
Carthage's power was broken after the Second Punic War, yet the Romans never forgave the city for Hannibal's invasion. In 150 B.C.E., the Carthaginians provided Rome with an excuse for a Third Punic War by attacking an ally of Rome, King Massinissa of Numidia. Even though Massinissa defeated the Carthaginians, the Romans attacked Carthage in 146 B.C.E. Its citizens were sold as slaves and the city was burned to the ground. Yet the site on the coast was too good to remain unoccupied, and the Romans later founded a city there.

ROMAN
EMPIRE
MACEDON
Philippi
Cynoscephalae 197 B.C.E.□
Thermopylae 191 B.C.E.
Corinth
Athens   □ Sardis
Magnesia 190 B.C.E.
Black Sea
Aral
Sea
Oxus
Caspian Sea
Mediterranean Sea
Crete
Rhodes
Cyprus
Antioch
Euphrates
Tigris
SELEUCID EMPIRE
PTOLEMAIC
KINGDOM
Alexandria
Babylon
Nile
Red Sea
Persian Gulf

Roman Empire and allies
Aetolian League
Achaean League
Kingdom of Pergamum
Macedon and allies
Independent Greek states
Ptolemaic kingdom
Seleucid Empire
■ **Roman victory**

▲ **THE HELLENISTIC EAST**
The three most powerful Hellenistic states were the Antigonid kingdom of Macedon, the Seleucid Empire of Syria and Iraq, and the Ptolemaic kingdom of Egypt. In Greece itself, there were two leagues of cities, the Aetolian League of northwestern Greece and the Achaean League of the south. Among smaller states was the kingdom of Pergamum in Asia Minor.

THE CONQUEST OF THE EAST

Victory in the Second Punic War (218-201 B.C.E.) turned Rome into a Mediterranean superpower, which ruled vast overseas territories. The Romans now became involved in the eastern Mediterranean, where there were various rival Hellenistic (Greek) kingdoms and leagues of cities. Increasingly, smaller Hellenistic states appealed to Rome for help against the larger kingdoms. The Romans were happy to intervene because they realized that it was in their own interests to weaken powerful neighbors. Yet because they were in awe of the civilization of Greece, the Romans always presented their eastern wars as campaigns fought on behalf of Greek freedom.

COIN OF
PHILIP V

▲ **PHILIP V**
Philip V was the ambitious king of Macedon, Italy's nearest neighbor among the Hellenistic states. He welcomed Hannibal's invasion of Italy, seeing his own chance to expand westward. In 215 B.C.E., he even signed a treaty with Hannibal. Backing Rome's deadliest enemy was a big mistake. Rome and Macedon were at war from 215 to 205 B.C.E., though little fighting took place because the Romans were occupied fighting Carthage.

◄ **CYNOSCEPHALAE**
In 200 B.C.E., after Hannibal had been dealt with, the Romans once again declared war on Philip. Three years later, the young Roman general Titus Quinctius Flamininus won a great victory over the Macedonians at Cynoscephalae. The Macedonians fought using a phalanx, a formation of tightly massed foot soldiers armed with long pikes called *sarissas*. This formation was unbeatable when attacking an enemy head on. However, using lessons learned from Hannibal at Cannae, Flamininus sent his soldiers to attack the undefended Macedonian flanks and rear.

◄ FREEDOM
Following his victory over Philip of Macedon, Flamininus attended the Isthmian Games, a great festival in Corinth, where delegations from the Greek kingdoms and cities came to meet him. Flamininus declared to the assembled people that Greece was now free, and that Rome did not wish to occupy any part of their country. This engraving shows him making the declaration at the Games. Grateful Greek cities quickly put up statues of the popular general, and gave him hundreds of gold crowns as gifts for Rome.

Doric columns

COIN OF FLAMININUS

Victoria, goddess of victory

TRIUMPH ►
Back in Rome, Flamininus celebrated with a triumphal procession, which lasted for three days—the greatest that had ever been held in the city. Flamininus rode through the city on a chariot, followed by his entire army. Carts were piled high with treasures, including bronze and marble statues, vases, silver shields, heaps of gold and silver, 14,514 Macedonian coins, and the gold crowns from the Greek cities. He had also taken many prisoners, including Philip's son Demetrius.

CORINTH DESTROYED ►
In spite of their promise that Greece was free, following a further war, the Romans went on to occupy Macedon in 168 B.C.E. They then began to interfere in the affairs of the Achaean League. This caused such bad feeling in Corinth, the League capital, that Roman envoys there were beaten up—an insult that Rome would not forgive. In 146 B.C.E., four legions captured Corinth. Although it was one of the most beautiful cities in Greece, Corinth was burned to the ground and her people sold into slavery. Greece became a Roman province. This is the Temple of Apollo, one of the few Greek buildings in Corinth that the Romans left standing.

conquest of the east

◄ WAR WITH ANTIOCHUS
While the Romans had been busy fighting Macedon, King Antiochus III of Syria had been expanding his empire, attacking the kingdom of Pergamum, an ally of Rome, and then invading Greece. Antiochus had also made himself an enemy of Rome by sheltering the exiled Hannibal. The Romans sent a new army, which defeated Antiochus at Thermopylae in Greece (191 B.C.E.) and at Magnesia in Asia Minor (190 B.C.E.). It was at Magnesia that Hannibal, fighting for Antiochus, was defeated for a second time by the Roman general Scipio Africanus.

ANTIOCHUS III

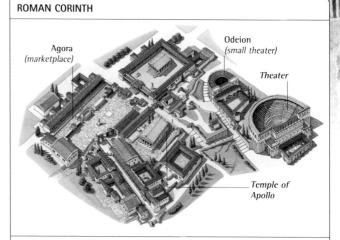

ROMAN CORINTH

Agora *(marketplace)*

Odeion *(small theater)*

Theater

Temple of Apollo

Corinth lay in ruins for more than a century. Then, in 44 B.C.E., it was refounded as a Roman city by the dictator, Julius Caesar, who remamed it Colonia Laus Iulia Corinthiensis ("Corinth the praise of Julius"). Corinth had always been ideally placed for trade and soon the Roman capital of southern Greece was as prosperous as ever.

CIVIL WARS

Warfare gave Rome's ambitious generals great opportunities to gain power, wealth, and glory. Each wanted to win lasting periods of command and to earn triumphal processions in Rome. For men like Julius Caesar, it was no longer enough to be consul for a single year. A new threat to the Republic came from the Roman soldiers, who expected to be given landholdings at the end of their service. The Senate was often reluctant to grant this, and so the soldiers came to depend on their generals to reward them. As a result, they often felt more loyalty for their generals than they did for the Roman state. In the 1st century B.C.E., growing conflict between the leading generals and the Senate led to a series of bitter civil wars, in which the republican system of government was destroyed.

▲ POMPEY THE GREAT
Gnaius Pompeius (106-48 B.C.E.), better known as Pompey, earned the nickname "the Great" following his campaigns against pirates in the Mediterranean, and King Mithridates of Pontus (now eastern Turkey). Back in Rome, in 59 B.C.E., he formed an alliance with two leading politicians, Julius Caesar and Crassus, who was the richest man in Rome. The three forced the Senate to give Caesar the consulship and Crassus an eastern command, and to provide Pompey's soldiers with landholdings in Italy.

◄ JULIUS CAESAR
After he was appointed consul, in 59 B.C.E., Julius Caesar took command of northern Italy and southern Gaul. Caesar saw this as his chance to outdo Pompey's achievements and, on his own initiative, he set out to conquer the whole of Gaul. The complete conquest took him seven years. He also led two daring expeditions to Britain, in 55 and 54 B.C.E. In the process, Caesar created a powerful army that was wholly loyal to him rather than to Rome. He also quarreled with many leading senators, who distrusted him and feared his growing power.

▲ CROSSING THE RUBICON
While Caesar was conquering Gaul, his enemies in the Senate had succeeded in turning Pompey against him. In 49 B.C.E., when Caesar's command was due to end, the Senate, led by Pompey, ordered him to hand over his army and return to Rome as a private citizen. Fearing his enemies in Rome, Caesar disobeyed the order and invaded Italy. This painting shows him leading his army over the Rubicon River—the southern boundary of his province. No commander was allowed to take his army outside his province without permission from the Senate, so this was an act of war. According to his biographer, Suetonius, a godlike figure appeared to Caesar at the Rubicon and led the way over the river. Caesar supposedly said, "Let us accept this as a sign from the gods, and follow where they beckon, in vengeance on our double-dealing enemies."

COIN OF CAESAR

KING IN ALL BUT NAME ▶

After further campaigns in which he defeated his remaining enemies, Caesar declared himself dictator for life in 44 B.C.E. He began to act like a king, sitting on a golden throne and issuing coins with his portrait on them—an honor previously reserved for famous Romans after death. A group of 60 senators, led by Brutus and Cassius, plotted to kill Caesar and restore the Republic. On March 15, 44 B.C.E., they surrounded him in Pompey's theater, where the Senate was meeting, and stabbed him to death. Caesar fell at the foot of Pompey's statue.

▲ WAR WITH THE SENATE

As Caesar marched through Italy, Pompey and many of the senators fled to Greece, where they raised a new army. Caesar followed and, in 48 B.C.E., he won a crushing victory over Pompey at the Battle of Pharsalus. Pompey fled to Alexandria in Egypt. As he stepped ashore, he was stabbed to death on the orders of the young king, Ptolemy, who hoped to win Caesar's gratitude. When Caesar arrived in pursuit of Pompey, he was presented with his head. Caesar burst into tears at the sight of his dead rival and former friend.

ANTONY

◀ ANTONY AND OCTAVIAN

Caesar's assassination did not save the Republic. It only led to further civil wars. His 18-year-old great-nephew and adopted heir, Octavian, raised a private army from Caesar's old soldiers and forced the Senate to make him consul, although he was more than 20 years too young. He then joined forces with Mark Antony, the other leading follower of Caesar. In 42 B.C.E., they defeated Caesar's assassins at Philippi in northeastern Greece, and made themselves joint rulers of the Empire. Octavian took the west while Antony ruled the east. To strengthen their partnership, Antony married Octavian's sister, Octavia.

OCTAVIAN

civil wars

ACTIUM ▶

In Egypt, Antony fell in love with Queen Cleopatra, and abandoned his wife Octavia for her. This outraged Octavian, and gave him the excuse to start a new civil war. In 31 B.C.E., he won a great sea battle over Antony at Actium, off the coast of Greece. Octavian pursued Antony and Cleopatra to Egypt, where they killed themselves. This relief of a Roman warship commemorates Octavian's victory. The crocodile on the ship is a symbol of Egypt, so the relief presents the defeat of Antony as a victory over a foreign enemy.

Wooden fighting turret

Crocodile carved in relief

AUGUSTUS

In 27 B.C.E., Octavian, who
had defeated all his rivals,
announced that he would restore
the republican system. He formally
handed control of the state back to
the Senate and the elected magistrates.
Octavian was now given a new name, Augustus ("the
revered one"). In reality, he gave up none of his power
because he kept overall command of Rome's armies, ruling
most of the important provinces. The Senate had little power,
yet Augustus made sure that it kept its traditional prestige.
Unlike Julius Caesar, who had made enemies by acting like
a king, Augustus lived simply, treating the senators with
respect. He had become Rome's first emperor.

Outstretched arm indicates he is making a speech

Breastplate

Augustus

IMPERIAL IMAGE ►
Augustus took great care over his public image. Although he
ruled for more than 40 years, his statues always showed him as
a handsome young man. Here he is dressed as a general with
bare feet—in art a sign of gods and heroes. At his right foot is
Cupid, son of Venus, a reminder that Augustus claimed to be
descended from this goddess. On his breastplate, a Parthian—an
eastern enemy of Rome—returns a captured standard. This was
the result of a treaty, yet Augustus claimed it as a victory.

Steps lead up to the altar

Religious procession winds around the sides

Cupid

Bare feet

Floral carving

MVNIF.PII.IX.P.M.
AN.XVIII

▲ AUGUSTUS THE BUILDER
Augustus won popular support by spending vast sums of money restoring Rome's
temples and putting up new buildings. He claimed to have found a city of brick
and left it marble. In 13 B.C.E., he built the Ara Pacis ("altar of peace") in Rome. This
celebrated the peace he had brought to the empire after years of civil war. The
altar itself stands inside this rectangular enclosure, whose outer walls are carved
with scenes of Augustus and his family in a religious procession.

▲ WIFE AND DAUGHTER

Members of Augustus's family were also portrayed in art with the features of gods. The figure at the front of this cameo is his daughter Julia, represented as Roma, the helmeted goddess of Rome. The other lady is Livia, his wife of 52 years, as Juno, goddess of women. Livia had a huge influence on Augustus, though she played the role of a traditional wife, and even spun and wove his clothes. Livia was the first Roman woman to be honored with public statues, and to be declared a goddess after death.

Red granite

THREE LEGIONS LOST

Augustus's coins record only his successes. He did not want people to remember the greatest disaster of his reign. This occurred in 9 B.C.E., when three Roman legions were ambushed and destroyed by Arminius, chieftain of the Cherusci tribe, in the Teutoberg forest of Germany. Almost 30,000 soldiers were killed, and their commander, Quinctilius Varus, committed suicide. Augustus had hoped to push the empire's frontier in Germany east to the Elbe River. Following the disaster, he had to withdraw to the Rhine, now fixed as a lasting frontier. In old age, Augustus was often heard to cry out in anguish, "Quinctilius Varus, give me back my legions!" This picture of the battle is by the 19th-century German artist, Friedrich Gunkel. To the Germans, Arminius (Hermann) is still a national hero.

◀ GIANT SUNDIAL

This is one of two Egyptian obelisks that Augustus brought back to Rome to remind people of his conquest of Egypt. The obelisk was used as the gnomon, or pointer, of a giant sundial. On the emperor's birthday, its shadow pointed directly to the center of the Ara Pacis.

ROMAN CALVARY MASK FOUND IN THE TEUTOBERG FOREST

POLITICAL PROPAGANDA

COINS

Augustus used his coins to spread information and to win support for his rule. On one side, he would have his portrait and titles. Those on this coin tell us that he was "Divi Filius" or son of a god (Julius Caesar), and that the Senate had awarded him the title of "Pater Patriae" (father of the country).

EGYPT CAPTURED

The reverse of each coin had a simple image representing an achievement, such as a victory in war. The chained crocodile shown on this coin represents Egypt, which Augustus had added to the Roman Empire in 30 B.C.E. Control of Egypt, with its fertile land, allowed Augustus to distribute free bread to the people of Rome.

TRIUMPHAL ARCH

This is a triumphal arch that Augustus had built in Orange, in Gaul (France). The arch was erected to commemorate the founding of the town, in 35 B.C.E., by retired soldiers who had served in Caesar's wars. It is a victory monument to Caesar's conquest of Gaul, which also brought prestige to his adopted son, Augustus.

CHIEF PRIEST

This statue of Augustus, with his head covered, shows his role as *Pontifex Maximus* (chief priest). He assumed this role in 13 B.C.E., on the death of the previous holder. The title provided the new position of emperor with religious dignity. For the next 400 years, every emperor who followed Augustus would also be chief priest.

HEIRS

Augustus planned that the imperial system would be continued after his death by his descendants. To get the Roman people used to the idea, he issued this coin in 2 B.C.E. It shows the coming of age of his grandsons, Gaius and Lucius, whom he had adopted as his heirs. Unfortunately, they both died before him.

EMPERORS

Augustus died in 14 C.E., after ruling for over 40 years.
Like Julius Caesar, he was declared a god after his death.
By now, Rome's upper classes had become used to the idea
of rule by one man. Although republican traditions had not
completely disappeared, the Senate offered the throne to
Augustus's stepson, Tiberius, who was later followed
by three other members of his family: Caligula,
Claudius, and Nero. They are known as the Julio-
Claudian dynasty (family of rulers). None of these
later rulers were to prove as successful or
popular as Augustus had been.

Oak-leaf wreath

STATUE OF CLAUDIUS DRESSED AS JUPITER

◄ GLOOMY TIBERIUS
Although an experienced
general, Tiberius (ruled
14-37 C.E.) had neither
expected nor wanted
to become emperor. He
was a gloomy and difficult man. Senators
felt uncomfortable in his presence, and he
had only contempt for them, describing
them as "men fit to be slaves." Scared of
assassination, Tiberius spent the last ten years
of his reign in retirement on the island of Capri,
off the west coast of Italy. In Rome, his death
was greeted with widespread relief. People took to
the streets shouting, "To the Tiber with Tiberius!"

INSANE EMPEROR ►
Tiberius was succeeded by Gaius (ruled
37-41 C.E.), who was nicknamed Caligula
("little boots"). He soon showed that he
was mentally unbalanced and unfit to rule.
Among other strange acts, he demanded to
be worshipped as a god and threatened
to make his favorite horse, Incitatus, a
consul. During his only military
campaign, in Germany, he
ordered his soldiers to
collect shells as "spoils of
the sea." Caligula was
murdered by his own
Praetorian Guards—the
soldiers in Rome who
were supposed
to protect the
emperor.

Eagle, Jupiter's sacred bird

emperors

▲ CLAUDIUS
The men of the Praetorian Guard, who had
assassinated Caligula, then chose his uncle
Claudius as emperor. Claudius (ruled 41-54 C.E.)
had been a figure of fun at Caligula's court,
mocked for his stammer, drooling, and nervous
tics. He was in fact intelligent, but needed a
spectacular military victory in order to improve
his image and strengthen his authority. So, in
43 C.E., he organized the invasion of Britain,
which became a new province of the empire.
He was the only member of the dynasty, after
Augustus, to be declared a god when he died.

OIL PAINTING OF NERO
PLAYING A GOLDEN LYRE

▲ NERO

The 16-year-old Nero (ruled 54-68 C.E.) followed Claudius on the throne. At first he was dominated by his mother, Agrippina, but as he grew older he wanted to break free of her influence. In 59 C.E., he had Agrippina stabbed to death. This left him free to follow his real interests—music and chariot racing. In 64 C.E., when a disastrous fire swept through Rome, Nero was said to have used the dramatic setting to sing songs and play his lyre. Many thought he had started the fire himself.

69 C.E. THE YEAR OF THE FOUR EMPERORS

GALBA

In 68-69 C.E., four emperors came to power in swift succession. The first was Galba, the 70-year-old governor of Spain, who had rebelled against Nero in April 68 C.E. Following Nero's suicide, in June, Galba was widely accepted as emperor. He arrived in Rome in the autumn, but would rule only until the following January 69 C.E.

OTHO

Otho had expected to be adopted as Galba's heir. When Galba chose another man, named Piso, Otho was furious. With the backing of the Praetorian Guard he had Galba and Piso murdered, seizing power in Rome. Meanwhile, the legions on the Rhine had declared their own general, Vitellius, emperor, and were marching on Italy.

VITELLIUS

In April 69 C.E. Otho's army was defeated by Vitellius at the Battle of Cremona. Otho killed himself, and Vitellius entered Rome as emperor. But by July, another rival, Titus Flavius Vespasian, had been proclaimed emperor by the legions in Egypt, Syria, and Judaea. A month later, the Danube legions also declared for Vespasian.

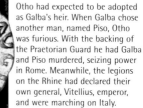

VESPASIAN

In September 69 C.E., Vespasian's troops defeated the Vitellians in a second battle at Cremona. In December, they fought their way into Rome, hunting down Vitellius, who was in hiding, and torturing him to death. Vespasian, the fourth emperor in a year, now founded a new dynasty, the Flavians, which would rule Rome for 26 years.

GOLDEN PALACE ▶

Following the fire, Nero seized a large area of the ruined city to build himself an enormous palace—the Domus Aurea ("Golden House"). On its completion, he declared, "At last I can live like a human being!" This made him deeply unpopular in Rome. The following year, when he discovered a plot against him, Nero had dozens of leading Romans executed. This led to a widespread rebellion in 68 C.E. Abandoned by almost everyone, Nero fled Rome and killed himself, saying, "What an artist the world is losing!"

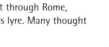

Key
1. Earlier Imperial palace (Palatine Hill)
2. Gilded bronze statue of Nero, 120 ft (37 m) high
3. Landscaped garden, also a private zoo
4. Colonnaded walkway
5. Ornamental pond
6. West wing of the palace (Esquiline Hill)

Extension built by Emperor Domitian

THE REMAINS OF THE IMPERIAL PALACE ON THE PALATINE HILL

Curved gallery, a walkway overlooking the Circus Maximus

▲ IMPERIAL PALACE
The wealthy lived in the hilltop districts, where the air was cleaner and there were fine views. The emperor himself lived in a great palace on the Palatine Hill, overlooking the Circus Maximus on one side, and the Forum on the other. Several emperors added new wings to the palace (from the word Palatine) until it covered the entire hill.

city of Rome

THE CITY OF ROME

In the 1st century C.E., Rome had a population of more than one million people. Many of them came from different lands, hoping to make their fortunes in the city they saw as the center of the world. Rome was full of huge public buildings, including temples, racetracks, theaters, bathhouses, basilicas (halls for law courts), and a great amphitheater for public shows. There were also 40 or more public parks and gardens stretching over the Esquiline and Pincian hills, and along the river. The city's aqueducts brought so much water into the city that, in the words of the writer Strabo, "veritable rivers flow through the city and the sewers."

◀ THE HEART OF THE CITY
This model shows the center of the city—the area between the Palatine and the Esquiline Hills. At the top is the Colosseum, a great amphitheater for public shows built by Emperor Vespasian and his sons. Two great aqueducts can be seen snaking their way through the city, bringing water to the city's many bathhouses and fountains. The Circus Maximus was the city's biggest racetrack.

Key

1. Forum
2. Temple of Venus and Roma
3. Colosseum
4. Imperial palaces
5. Aqueduct of Nero
6. Temple of Emperor Claudius
7. Circus Maximus
8. Aqua Marcia Aqueduct

Extension built by Septimius Severus

INSULAE

Space was scarce, so Rome had narrow streets and tall buildings, some up to 70 ft (21 m) high. The city was divided into blocks called *insulae* ("islands"). This surviving street in Ostia, Rome's earliest port, shows what the lowest levels of an *insula* looked like, with well-built brick walls. Higher levels were usually less well constructed, using timber and rubble. The poorest people lived in the upper floors, where they had farther to climb and were more at risk of being trapped in a fire.

▲ DANGERS

With upper floors made of wood, and oil lamps and open fires in braziers used for warmth, *insulae* were a constant fire hazard. The worst fire of all took place in 64 C.E. and burned for five days, destroying ten of Rome's 14 districts. Buildings often fell down without warning because they were so tall, and badly built. The poet Juvenal, who lived in Rome, wrote that he would prefer "to live where fires and midnight panics are not quite such common events."

ANCIENT ROME TODAY

THE FORUM
No other capital city has as many preserved ancient ruins in its center as Rome. This is the Forum, ancient Rome's center for government, law, and religion. To the left of the picture is the triumphal arch of Emperor Septimius Severus. The tall red building in the center is the Curia Julia, where the Senate met.

PIAZZA NAVONA
Not only ruins, but the very outline of the streets reveal the ancient city beneath the modern one. The Piazza Navona gets its long, narrow shape and rounded ends because it was originally a *circus* (racetrack) built by Emperor Domitian. The Egyptian obelisk in the background was specially built for him in Egypt.

MAUSOLEUM OF AUGUSTUS
This is the mausoleum of Emperor Augustus, which he had built as a tomb for his whole family. It was surrounded by a park laid out with walks. Although the mausoleum is now plain brick, it was once faced with gleaming white marble. The top of the mausoleum was covered with earth and planted with evergreen trees.

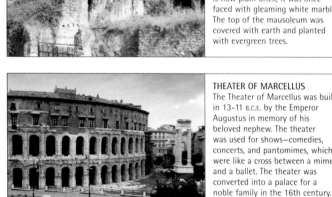

THEATER OF MARCELLUS
The Theater of Marcellus was built in 13-11 B.C.E. by the Emperor Augustus in memory of his beloved nephew. The theater was used for shows—comedies, concerts, and pantomimes, which were like a cross between a mime and a ballet. The theater was converted into a palace for a noble family in the 16th century.

HADRIAN'S MAUSOLEUM
The vast Castel Sant' Angelo was originally another imperial mausoleum, built by Emperor Hadrian when Augustus's became full. Antoninus Pius, Hadrian, Commodus, Marcus Aurelius, Septimius Severus, and Caracalla all had their ashes placed here. The bridge, called the Pons Aelius, was also built by Hadrian.

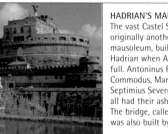

TIBER ISLAND
The Tiber Island is linked to the city on the right by Rome's oldest surviving bridge, the Pons Fabricius, built in 62 B.C.E. A church dedicated to St. Bartholomew now stands on the foundations of a temple to Aesculapius, the ancient Greek god of healing. A modern hospital continues the island's ancient healing tradition.

THE FORUM

Rome's chief public square, the Forum, was the center for the city's government, law, business, and religion. It was surrounded by important temples and public buildings, including the Senate House, the public records office, and two great law courts. Along one side, and lined with statues of Rome's most famous men, ran the Via Sacra ("sacred road"), which was used for triumphal and religious processions. Other monuments included triumphal arches and the Golden Milestone, from which the Romans—who regarded the Forum as the center of the world—measured all distances to Rome. On a smaller scale, every Roman town had its own forum for local government.

Forum

THE FORUM TODAY ▶
This view shows Rome's Forum as it looks today, photographed from the southwest. From these scattered remains, it is hard to imagine that this was once the heart of the Mediterranean world. The careful preservation of the Forum's ruins shows just how important this place still is to the Italians.

Temple of Vespasian and Titus

Curia (Senate House)

Triumphal Arch of Septimius Severus

THE FORUM IN THE TIME OF AUGUSTUS

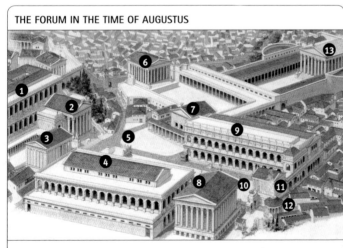

1. Tabularium, Rome's public records office
2. Temple of Concord, dedicated to harmonious agreement
3. Temple of Saturn
4. Basilica Julia, law court begun by Julius Caesar and completed by Augustus
5. Rostra, platform for making public speeches
6. Temple of Venus, the goddess whom Augustus claimed as his ancestor

7. Curia, where the Senate met
8. Temple of Castor and Pollux, twin gods supposed to have helped Rome win a battle in 484 B.C.E.
9. Basilica Aemilia, law court built in 179 B.C.E.
10. Triumphal Arch erected in 19 B.C.E.
11. Temple of Julius Caesar
12. Temple of Vesta, goddess of the hearth
13. Temple of Mars the Avenger

◀ CURIA
The Senate met in the hall called the Curia Julia, which is the best-preserved building in the Forum. The reason it has survived is that it was converted into a church in the 7th century C.E. Originally built by, and named after, Julius Caesar, the Curia was later restored by the emperors Domitian and Diocletian. From the time of Augustus, it also served as a law court, where major trials were held.

TABULARIUM ▶
This is the Tabularium or public records office. It held a vast collection of official documents, including laws, emperors' decrees, advice to the emperor from the Senate, election results, documents relating to the foundation of colonies, and treaties with foreign states. The upper levels, with lighter walls, were added in the Middle Ages, when the building was converted into a palace.

Temple of Saturn

Temple of Antoninus
Pius and Faustina

Via Sacra

ORATOR ▶
This is a statue of Quintilian
(c.35–c.95 C.E.), a famous
orator (public speaker),
who often spoke in law
cases in the basilicas of the
Forum. He also taught the
skills of public speaking, and
wrote a famous book *Training
in Oratory*, in which he
gives advice on how to win
over a jury by rousing their
emotions or making them
laugh. Though Romans were
able to speak on their own
behalf in law cases, they
would often hire a skilled
speaker such as Quintilian
to put their case for them.
Such a professional pleader
was called an advocate.

◀ BASILICA JULIA
This is all that remains of the
Basilica Julia, the great law
court begun by Julius Caesar.
This basilica specialized in
sorting out disputes over wills
and inheritance. Hearings were
often crowded and noisy, for
each side in a case would pack
the halls with supporters to
cheer their own speeches, and
hiss those of the other side.
Many came for entertainment,
for the cases often involved
scandals among the rich.

THE ROSTRA ▶
At one end of the Forum
there was a speaker's
platform known as the Rostra
("beaks"). The name derives
from the bronze beaks of
warships, captured in a sea
battle against Antium in
338 B.C.E, that were displayed
here. This is the origin of our
word "rostrum," meaning a
speaker's platform. Funeral
speeches praising famous
Romans, such as Julius Caesar,
were given here.

▲ PUNISHMENTS
To the west of the Senate House, there is an underground prison. Convicted
criminals awaiting execution were held here. Upper-class Romans had the
privilege of a private execution by beheading. This is the origin of the term
"capital punishment," from the Latin *caput* ("head"). Lower-class Romans were
given a painful and humiliating public execution. They might be thrown to
wild animals in an amphitheater, flogged to death, or nailed to a cross.

THE AMPHITHEATER

Most large Roman towns had an amphitheater—a round, open-air building, where gladiators, usually slaves or condemned criminals, fought to the death to entertain vast, cheering crowds. These shows were staged by Rome's rulers, at great expense, as a way of winning popularity. In Rome, the shows were a strong unifying force. They gave the people a chance to see their emperor and to share an exciting experience with him. They also allowed the emperor to display his power—he decided whether a defeated gladiator should live or die.

Colosseum is 170 ft (52 m) high

COLOSSEUM ▶
The Colosseum, Rome's largest amphitheater, was built by Emperor Vespasian and his sons on the site of Nero's palace. The immense structure could hold more than 50,000 spectators, who sat in rows according to their social position. The emperor and the senators sat on the podium at the front, while less important men sat further back, and women and slaves were at the top. There were 80 entrances at ground level: 76 for ordinary spectators, two for the imperial family, and two for gladiators. There was a vast network of underground tunnels and cages where wild animals, such as lions and tigers, were held.

GLADIATORS

THE NET MAN
There were around 20 different types of gladiator, distinguished by their weapons, costumes, and method of combat. The *retiarius*, or net man, was armed like a fisherman with a net and a trident—a spear with three prongs. He would throw his net at an opponent to trap him, and then spear him with his trident.

SECUTOR
The *retiarius* usually fought against a *secutor* ("pursuer"), who wore a smooth egg-shaped helmet with two round eye-holes. This was specially designed so that it would not get caught in his opponent's net. The *secutor* was armed with a sword and carried a long shield to protect him from the trident.

THRACIAN
The Thracian had armor and weapons based on those used by Rome's enemies in Thrace (modern Bulgaria). He carried a curved sword, called a *sica*, and a small shield, and wore a large wide-brimmed helmet with a grid at the front. The Gaul and Samnite were two other types of gladiator based on traditional enemies of Rome.

amphitheater

Thracian gladiator

GLADIATORS AT HOME ▶
Throughout the empire, people decorated their homes with mosaics and wall paintings showing gladiatorial fights. The same scenes also appear on everyday items, such as vases, oil lamps, and cutlery. Even babies' bottles had gladiators pictured on them. It was thought that the baby would drink in the gladiator's strength with the milk.

OIL LAMP

▲ APPEAL FOR MERCY

This vase from Britain may be a souvenir of a real fight, because the gladiators are named. Valentinus, the defeated *retiarius*, raises a finger, to appeal to the crowd for mercy. Depending on his performance, the crowd would shout "Spare him!" or "Finish him off!" Memnon, the victorious *secutor*, holds his sword raised, waiting for the crowd's verdict.

▲ EXECUTIONS

The amphitheater was also the arena for public executions. Criminals were tied to stakes to be torn apart by wild beasts, such as lions or tigers. Mosaics showing such grisly scenes would often be found in homes, an indication of just how bloodthirsty the Romans were. They believed that it was a good thing to kill criminals, and they enjoyed watching it done.

▲ WILD ANIMALS

Wild animals, such as leopards, bears, and ostriches, were brought to amphitheaters from all over the empire to be displayed or killed by trained beast fighters. This was a public demonstration of Rome's conquest of wild nature. Some animals were let loose on prisoners, while others, such as elephants, performed dances and wrote letters in the sand.

Brick and concrete walls, faced with limestone

COMMODUS ▶

Emperor Commodus was so obsessed with gladiators that he became one himself, even moving into the gladiators' barracks. He appeared in the Colosseum, dressed as Hercules, and chased and killed ostriches.

Lion skin associated with Hercules

GLADIATOR GRAFFITI

Although gladiators came from the lowest classes, they were as popular as football stars today. Evidence of this adulation is seen in the drawings of gladiators scratched on walls by fans. In Pompeii, one piece of graffiti carries the words, "Celadus the Thracian makes the girls sigh."

CHARIOT RACING

The most popular and exciting Roman spectator sport was chariot racing, which took place in a track called a *circus*, named after its oval shape. The most famous of these was the Circus Maximus in Rome, but racetracks have been found across the Roman empire. As many as 24 races could take place in one day. The historian Ammianus Marcellinus described the attitude of race-goers in Rome: "The center of all their hopes and desires is the Circus Maximus ... On the longed-for day of the races they rush headlong to the course before the first glimmering of dawn as if they would outstrip the competing teams, most of them having passed a sleepless night."

Charioteer whips the horses on

Chariots were light and made of wood

Starting gates

Obelisk

Metae

Spina

Stands

CIRCUS MAXIMUS ►
Rome's Circus Maximus was 1,968 ft (600 m) long, and could hold around 250,000 spectators—five times more than the Colosseum. The western end held 12 boxes or stalls, where the chariots waited behind metal starting gates. A 1,130-ft (344-m)-long barrier called the *spina* (spine) ran down the middle of the track. This was decorated with statues and monuments, including two Egyptian obelisks. The chariots raced around the *spina* in a counterclockwise direction, turning at posts called *metae*.

THE RACE

RIVAL TEAMS
The charioteers belonged to rival teams named after four colors—green, red, white, and blue. Each had its own stables, trainers, grooms, and horses. Like today's sports fans, people cheered for their teams and gambled on them winning. Some took it so seriously that they even tried to put a curse on other teams.

THE RACE BEGINS
The race began at a signal from a magistrate (the large figure, *top left*), who dropped a white flag called a *mappa*. The iron starting gates sprung open and the chariots burst out. Drivers had to stay within their lanes until they reached a "break point" when they could then start to jostle for position.

JOSTLING FOR POSITION
The charioteers jostled for position, hoping to get as close as possible to the *spina* to ensure the shortest route around the turn, which was the most dangerous part of the race. Each charioteer wrapped the reins around his waist, bracing his body to avoid being thrown out, and steered by shifting his weight.

STAR CHARIOTEERS ▶

Although they were of low social status—often slaves or slaves who had won their freedom (freedmen)—charioteers became great stars. This mosaic from a bathhouse shows Polydus, a star charioteer from the red team, whose color he wears. His lead horse, Compressor ("Crusher"), is also named, for horses were often as famous as charioteers. In the 1st century C.E., the most famous charioteer in Rome was Scorpus, who won 2,048 races before he was killed, at the age of just 26. He was celebrated in a poem by Martial: "I am Scorpus, the glory of the noisy Circus, the much-applauded and short-lived darling of Rome."

A palm of victory

Compressor leads the other horses

Four-horse chariot called a quadriga

▲ CONTROLLING THE HORSES

This bronze model shows how a charioteer controlled his horses. Each horse had a pair of reins, which the charioteer wrapped around his body, and held in his left hand. He then steered by shifting his weight, tugging on the reins, and also used a whip to drive the team on. He carried a short, curved knife in his tunic, which he might use to cut himself free if he was thrown from the chariot. Sometimes special races were held with six or even eight horses to a team.

chariot racing

THE TURN

At the far end of the track there were tall turning posts (gilded bronze cones in Rome) called *metae*, where chariots often crashed into each other or were overturned. Here one charioteer has had an accident and his horses lie in a heap on the ground. Such an accident was called a *naufragium*, from the Latin for a shipwreck.

EGGS AND DOLPHINS

Each race usually lasted for seven laps. These were counted by removing large wooden eggs or turning over models of dolphins positioned on the *spina*. According to the Christian writer Tertullian, the dolphins were there in honor of Neptune, god of horses as well as of the sea. Dolphins were also considered the fastest of all creatures.

VICTORY PALM

The winning charioteer received a symbolic palm of victory, as well as prize money, which could bring successful charioteers great wealth. The Roman writer Juvenal complained that a charioteer could earn a hundred times the fee of a lawyer, while the poet Martial described Scorpus winning 15 bags of gold in an hour.

BATHHOUSES

Every Roman town or city had a bathhouse for the local people. More than just somewhere to wash, this was a recreation center and a place to relax and meet friends, often in the afternoon. In Rome there were five great bathhouses, built by a series of emperors in order to win popularity. One of the largest was built by Caracalla, who ruled 211–217 C.E. His baths, the towering ruins of which still stand in Rome, could hold 1,500 people.

▲ CARACALLA
Caracalla was a ruthless man who murdered his own brother, Geta, in order to take power. He also killed thousands of Geta's supporters. Statues of Caracalla show him scowling threateningly and giving a suspicious sidelong glance. He was eventually assassinated.

ART GALLERY ►
Caracalla's bathhouse doubled as an art gallery, where visitors could admire large copies of famous Greek sculptures. This copy of *The Farnese Bull*, a work in bronze from the 1st century B.C.E. by Apollonius, tells the story of Dirce, a cruel woman who was tied to an angry bull by Ampheon and Zethus to avenge their mother, Antiope.

Bull

Dirce

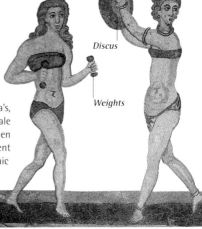

WOMEN ►
Women visited the baths separately from men. In large bath houses, such as Caracalla's, there were separate male and female areas. In small bath houses, men and women went at different times of the day. This mosaic shows two young Sicilian women doing lifting and throwing exercises.

Discus

Weights

VISITING THE BATHS

APODYTERIUM
Visitors to the baths first made their way to the *apodyterium* ("changing room"). This is the women's changing room in the baths in Herculaneum. They undressed here, leaving their clothes on the shelves. Thefts were quite common, so bathers often brought their own slave or hired one at the baths to look after their belongings.

EXERCISE
Once they had undressed, the bathers could swim in the pool, or go to the *palaestra* ("wrestling ground") to exercise. After rubbing themselves with oil, men and women might play ball games or lift weights. Men also ran races, wrestled, and boxed, protecting their hands with leather thongs, like the two naked boxers here.

▲ BATHWATER
Water was brought to Caracalla's baths from springs 56 miles (90 km) away along the Aqua Marcia aqueduct. It flowed into a huge cistern and then to the main building, where pipes carried it directly to the cold pools, or to boilers over wood furnaces where it was heated for the warm and hot baths.

▲ HEATING
Caracalla's baths had at least 50 furnaces, some to heat the water and others to heat the rooms using a hot-air system called the hypocaust. Floors rested on columns of brick or stone, leaving spaces for the hot air to pass between. This also flowed through terra-cotta pipes inside the walls.

▲ TOILETS
There were also communal toilets, where people sat side by side on cold marble seats. They wiped themselves with sponges on sticks they rinsed in the narrow channel of water that flowed at their feet. Water running down drains underneath the benches would flush waste away into the sewers.

Columns of pink Breccia marble

Open-air swimming pool surrounded on three sides by porticos

HOT ROOM
After exercising, bathers might go to the *caldarium* ("hot room"), where they had a steam bath to open up their pores. This hot room from the baths in Pompeii includes a *labrum*, a basin with cool water with which the men could splash themselves. Some bathhouses had a *laconicum*, which provided dry heat like a sauna.

OIL AND STRIGIL
The Romans did not have soap. Instead they covered their bodies with olive oil, which was often scented. This was then scraped away, along with the dirt, using a curved bronze tool called a strigil, two of which are shown here. Slaves would be on hand to do this, and to give massages and other beauty treatments.

COLD ROOM
After sweating in the *caldarium*, bathers cooled off in the *frigidarium* ("cold room"). This *frigidarium* from the baths in Pompeii has a round pool that would have been filled with cold water so bathers could jump in for a refreshing plunge. Romans believed that cold baths were good for the health.

▲ SWIMMING POOL
The Romans loved to swim, for exercise and fun. This large, open-air *natatio* ("swimming pool") was part of the imperial bath complex built by Emperor Hadrian in 127 C.E. in Lepcis Magna, in North Africa. Today the pool's water is green with algae and no longer fit to swim in, but in Roman times there was a constant flow of water through the pool, which kept it clean. The old water flowed out to other parts of the bath complex, while clean, fresh water flowed in.

bath houses

LIBRARIES AND BOOKS

Libraries were invented by the Greeks, and the earliest Roman examples were modeled on famous Greek libraries in Pergamum and Alexandria. Roman libraries had collections of Greek as well as Latin books, because every well educated Roman could read Greek. The books were in the form of scrolls, which were stored in boxes to protect them from moths and dust. The biggest libraries held up to 500,000 scrolls, about the equivalent of 100,000 modern books. The larger bathhouses, such as those of Emperor Caracalla, often had libraries and reading rooms, providing free access to books.

libraries and books

◄ PAPYRUS
Scrolls were made from an Egyptian marsh plant called papyrus—the origin of our word paper. To make sheets, thin strips of papyrus were soaked with water and woven together on a wooden board, the plant's natural starch acting as a sort of glue. Scenes showing the worship of the sun god, Re, appear on this papyrus from Roman Egypt.

◄ READING A BOOK
This wall painting from Herculaneum shows how a Roman would read a scroll. The text was written in columns. After finishing a column, the reader would roll it up with the left hand while unrolling the scroll in the right hand, revealing a new column. Romans usually read aloud, which must have made libraries noisy places.

BOOKS WITH PAGES ►
Papyrus was expensive, so people usually wrote notes on a wooden tablet coated with wax, using a *stylus*. This painting shows a woman with a notebook with four separate tablets, which could be turned like pages. In the 1st century B.C.E., this led to the invention of the *codex*, or book, with separate pages made of parchment (sheepskin), a stronger material than papyrus. The advantage of a *codex* was that a reader could quickly flip through its pages to find a particular passage. It might take hours to look through a scroll. *Codices* were also much easier to carry around.

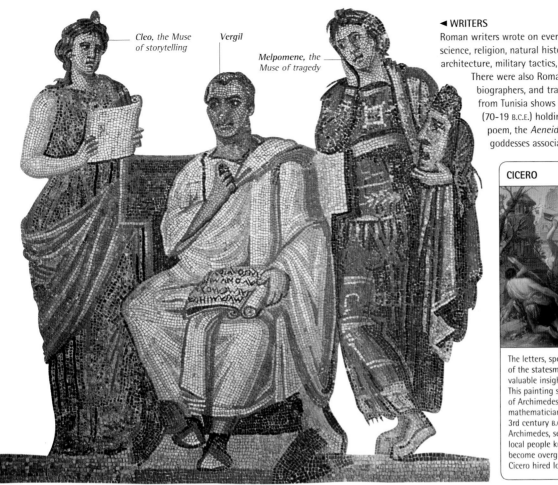

Cleo, the Muse of storytelling

Vergil

Melpomene, the Muse of tragedy

◄ WRITERS

Roman writers wrote on every possible subject, including science, religion, natural history, farming, medicine, architecture, military tactics, and water management. There were also Roman poets, historians, biographers, and travel writers. This mosaic from Tunisia shows Rome's greatest poet Vergil (70-19 B.C.E.) holding a copy of his most famous poem, the *Aeneid*. He is flanked by two Muses, goddesses associated with the arts.

CICERO

The letters, speeches, and philosophical writings of the statesman Cicero (c.106-43 B.C.E.) provide a valuable insight into life in Republican Rome. This painting shows Cicero's discovery of the tomb of Archimedes, a famous Greek inventor and mathematician who lived in Syracuse, Sicily, in the 3rd century B.C.E. In 75 B.C.E., Cicero, who admired Archimedes, set out to find his tomb, which the local people knew nothing about. The tomb had become overgrown with brambles and thorns and Cicero hired local men to clear them away.

WRITING MATERIALS

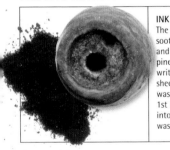

INK
The Romans made black ink using soot mixed with water or vinegar, and gum—a sticky resin from pine trees. This could be used for writing on papyrus or on thin sheets of wood. This blue inkpot was made in Egypt in the 1st century C.E. Ink was poured into the large hole and the pen was dipped into the smaller one.

WAX AND STYLUS
Beeswax was melted and poured into shallow cavities in wooden tablets to form a reusable writing surface. The three tools shown here are bronze, iron, and ivory *styli*, with pointed tips for writing on the wax tablets. The flat end of the *stylus* was used to wipe the wax smooth so that the writer could begin a new message.

STONE
The most lasting writing material was stone, so this was chosen by people for carved tomb inscriptions. This tombstone, from Roman Britain, is a memorial to four soldiers who belonged to the seventh and twenty-second legions. The large "D M" at the top is short for *Dis Manibus*, meaning "To the spirits of the dead."

LITERARY EMPERORS ►

Several emperors were also writers. Domitian (right) wrote poetry as well as a manual called "On the Care of the Hair." The emperor, who felt sensitive about his own thinning hair, wrote on the opening page, "Nothing is more pleasing than beauty, but nothing shorter-lived." Another literary emperor was Claudius, who wrote histories in Greek of the Carthaginians and the Etruscans. Claudius gave public readings from his books, despite being handicapped by a bad stammer. However, he gave up after an embarrassing incident when a bench collapsed beneath an overweight member of his audience.

◄ LIBRARY OF CELSUS

This magnificent library in Ephesus in Turkey was built in 135 C.E. by Julius Aquila as a monument to his father, Celsus Polemaeanus. Celsus, who had been governor of the province and a great lover of books, was buried beneath the floor of the library in a marble tomb. His son also provided money for the purchase of more than 12,000 scrolls.

Statue is one of many representing wisdom, knowledge, intelligence, and virtue

ARCHITECTURE

"In great buildings, as well as in other things, the rest of the world has been outdone by us Romans," wrote Pliny the Elder. The Romans invented concrete, which enabled them to build stronger and bigger structures than ever before. Their other main building material was brick, which they mass-produced in vast quantities. Unlike Greek temples, which were built with carved stones, a typical Roman temple was made of concrete and brick. Yet the Romans admired Greek architecture, borrowing its styles and hiring Greek architects. They even made their buildings look like Greek temples from the outside, by facing them with stone.

▲ AQUEDUCTS
Built around 19 B.C.E., this mighty Roman bridge spans the Gard River in France. It was part of a 30-mile (50-km)-long aqueduct that carried water to the town of Nîmes. The Pont du Gard, which stands 160 ft (49 m) tall, was built on three levels, with the water conduit at the top of the third level. Constructed entirely without mortar, the bridge's stones, some of which weigh up to six tons, are held together with iron clamps.

Inscription commemorates Emperors Titus and Vespasian

Composite (mixed) columns, with Corinthian leaves with Ionic scrolls

ARCHES ▶
It was possible to build vast bridges thanks to the use of the arch, a curved structure spanning an open space. A wall with arches is as strong as a solid one but much quicker to build. It is also lighter, so does not require such deep foundations. The Romans used arches for the outer walls of theaters and amphitheaters. They also built triumphal arches, decorative gateways serving as victory monuments. This is the Arch of Titus in Rome, the oldest surviving triumphal arch, built in 81 C.E.

▲ CONCRETE
Roman concrete was made of rubble mixed with mortar made from lime (burnt chalk or limestone), volcanic ash, and water. The mortar held the concrete together, while the rubble gave it strength. Here the concrete and brick core of the Colosseum is exposed.

▲ MIXED WORK
This wall uses a building method called *opus mixtum* ("mixed work"), which combines alternating courses of red bricks and stones with panels of small stone blocks set in diagonal lines in cement. Such panels were liable to crack. The brick courses stopped the cracks spreading.

architecture

▲ MAN-POWERED CRANE
The Romans used man-powered cranes to lift heavy building materials, as can be seen in this tomb carving belonging to a family who may have worked as building contractors. Slaves are shown walking inside the wheel.

GREEK COLUMNS

DORIC
There were three different styles of Greek column, which the Romans copied. Buildings such as the Colosseum incorporated all three styles on different levels. This column is in the sturdy, plain Doric style.

IONIC
The capitals (tops) of Ionic columns are decorated with spirals at the corners, each resembling a loosely rolled papyrus scroll. These are known as *volutes*, from the Latin word for scroll.

CORINTHIAN
This was the latest and most elaborate of the three styles, with the capitals ornately decorated with acanthus leaves. The Romans used this style on a much greater scale than the Greeks.

Arch is more than 50 ft (15 m) high

Marble imported from Athens in Greece

▲ VAULTS
The Romans learned to build a row of arches to make a barrel vault—a ceiling shaped like half a tube. Four barrel vaults meeting at right angles could then be used to make a crossvault. As their methods improved, Roman builders created larger and lighter interior spaces.

▲ DOMES
A number of arches, repeated in a circle, could also be used to make a dome. For the first time, a large interior space could be built without dozens of columns to hold up the ceiling. This is the dome of the Pantheon, built by Emperor Hadrian as a temple to all the gods. The concrete dome has 140 decorative, square coffers (recesses), shown here, which help reduce the ceiling's weight.

ROMAN ART

The Romans were great lovers of art, in particular the art of the Greeks, many of whose sculptures and paintings they seized and brought back to Rome. From the 1st century B.C.E., many Greek artists moved to Rome and other western cities to seek work. Almost all the sculptors from the Roman period whose names we know were Greeks. While the Romans imitated earlier Greek art, they also developed new forms of their own. The best known of these is the mosaic—a picture made from hundreds of tiny tiles called *tesserae.*

▲ GLASSWARE

One Roman invention was the glass cameo, a relief carving in different layers of colored glass. A glassblower made this vase using dark blue glass wrapped in an outer layer of white glass. Then a sculptor carved the figures, cutting away the white layer to reveal the darker layer beneath. One of only 13 complete cameo vases to survive, this vase was smashed into 200 pieces in 1845 by a visitor to London's British Museum. Although it has been carefully repaired, the cracks are still visible.

Statue's head is 8½ ft (2.6 m) tall

COLOSSAL STATUES ▶

Giant statues like this, made in bronze or stone, were called *colossi.* This marble head belonged to a statue of Emperor Constantine. The sculpture showed Constantine seated on a throne holding a globe in one hand, symbolizing his claim to rule the world. Only the head, arms, and feet were made of marble. The body, which has not survived, was probably a wooden frame covered with bronze or plaster.

◄ MARBLE AND PORPHYRY

The Roman empire provided sculptors with a variety of colored stone, which they combined to make statues. This is a sculpture of a captive barbarian, an enemy of Rome. His beard and long hair mark him out as a barbarian. Such statues were erected by the Romans as victory monuments. His arms and head are made of Italian marble, while his clothing is carved from porphyry, a beautiful purple stone found in the Egyptian desert. Only the body here is Roman. The head was added by the Italian sculptor Pietro Bernini (1562–1629), who admired ancient Roman art, and restored many sculptures.

art

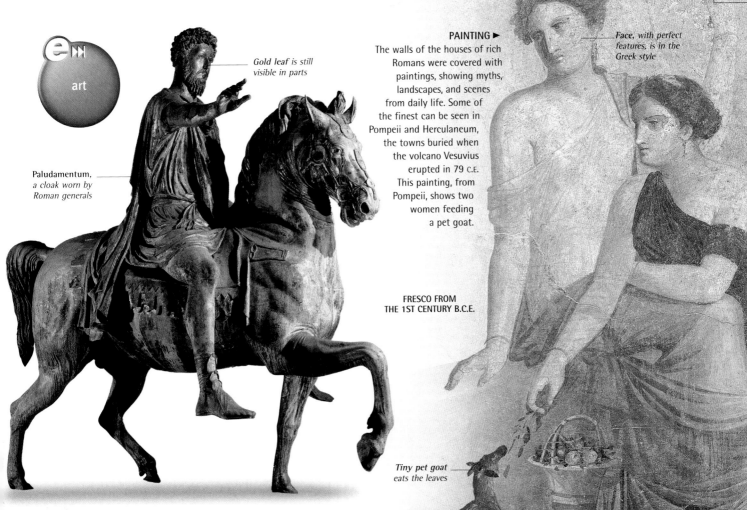

Gold leaf is still visible in parts

Paludamentum, a cloak worn by Roman generals

PAINTING ▶
The walls of the houses of rich Romans were covered with paintings, showing myths, landscapes, and scenes from daily life. Some of the finest can be seen in Pompeii and Herculaneum, the towns buried when the volcano Vesuvius erupted in 79 C.E. This painting, from Pompeii, shows two women feeding a pet goat.

Face, with perfect features, is in the Greek style

FRESCO FROM THE 1ST CENTURY B.C.E.

Tiny pet goat eats the leaves

▲ BRONZE STATUES
This bronze statue of Emperor Marcus Aurelius was made by the lost wax process. The sculptor carved a model from wax and then encased it in clay. This was then baked so that the wax melted, leaving behind a hollow, clay mold. Molten bronze was then poured into the mold, filling the space left by the "lost" wax. After the bronze had cooled and hardened, the mold was smashed open to reveal the statue. Molten bronze is very heavy, so large statues like this one, which is 11½ft (3.5 m) tall, had to be made in small sections, which were then joined together. The statue was originally covered in gold leaf, and must have been a dazzling sight.

◀ MOSAICS
Of all Roman art forms, mosaics have survived in the largest numbers. This is because they were used to decorate floors, which are often the only part of a Roman building to survive. Similar pictures and patterns are repeated in mosaics from different countries. This suggests that the craftsmen may have had catalogs from which people could choose their favorite design. This pavement mosaic shows the Medusa, a frightening monster from a Greek myth who had writhing snakes growing from her head instead of hair.

DINING-ROOM MOSAIC

One of the most unusual mosaics was made for Emperor Hadrian's dining room in his palace in Tibur (Tivoli) outside Rome. Signed by a Greek called Heracleitos, it is a picture of a white floor, on which fish bones, shells, fruit stones, and other leftovers from a meal lie scattered, all casting shadows. The scraps, which have become decorative in their own right, serve as a reminder of the delicious meals that have gone before. The idea of a floor decorated with a floor probably appealed to Hadrian's sense of humor.

POMPEII

On the morning of August 24, 79 C.E., Mount Vesuvius, a volcano that towers over the Bay of Naples, suddenly erupted, sending up a thick cloud of ash, pumice (volcanic stone), and poisonous gases. Within hours, Pompeii, the prosperous town built in the shadow of the volcano, had been completely buried. An eyewitness, Pliny the Younger, who saw the eruption from the safety of Misenum to the north, watched in horror as a dense, black cloud covered the sky. He wrote, "darkness fell as if a lamp had been put out in a closed room." This was the greatest natural disaster that Europe had ever seen. Yet the pumice and ash that engulfed the town of Pompeii also preserved it. Streets, houses, stores, and even people were frozen in time, just as they were on that fateful summer's day.

VESUVIUS ▶
This is Pompeii today, seen from the south, with Mount Vesuvius looming in the background. The top of the volcano was blown away by the eruption, leaving a crater 7 miles (11 km) in circumference. The long, straight road was one of three main roads running through Pompeii. In the foreground are the town's two theaters.

Vesuvius

◄ WRITING ON THE WALL

The walls of Pompeii are covered with writing, including love messages, advertisements, jokes, and insults. One person wrote simply, "I've caught a cold," while another joked, "I am surprised, oh wall, that having to carry so many stupid writings, you can still stand up." Candidates in local elections, or their supporters, had notices, such as this one, painted on their houses, urging people to vote for them.

Pompeii

Sunken container for food

Family shrine (lararium)

▲ SNACK BAR

This is a *thermopolium*, or snack bar, where the people of Pompeii would come to grab a quick bite to eat and drink a cup of wine as they went about their business in the town. Hot food was kept in sunken terracotta containers (*dolia*) in the masonry counter. There were no seats, so the customers leaned on the counter as they ate. This was also the home of the owner, whose household shrine is painted on the wall. Here he would make offerings to the gods who protected his business and home. They include Bacchus, god of wine, and Mercury, god of trade. Archeologists discovered the remains of a cloth bag containing the previous day's takings, which the owner had hidden in a *dolium* for safe keeping.

BODY CASTS

CASTS OF VICTIMS

The Italian archeologist Giuseppe Fiorelli began excavating the town in 1860. The victims' bodies, which had been sealed in the ash, had left spaces when they had decomposed. Fiorelli devised the technique of injecting plaster into these spaces to create lifelike models. This cast is of a man found lying in the street, leaning on one arm. He was buried so quickly by the ashes that he had died before he had time to lie down.

DOG

Animals as well as humans suffered on the day Vesuvius erupted. Here, afraid and writhing in agony from the burning ash, is a guard dog still wearing its collar. The dog's body was found inside the entrance hall of the house of Vesonius Primus. Its head is twisted back, pulled by the chain which still attached it to the wall. Unlike many casts, this one is so detailed that the dog's teeth can be seen.

IN THE GARDEN

A group of terrified adults and children were killed in a garden belonging to a rich Pompeiian called Marcus Lucretius. They had covered their faces in a desperate attempt to avoid breathing in the poisonous gases. Among them were a mother with a baby, and a girl who had buried her face in a man's clothing. These casts were made in 1966. Others casts have been made of furniture, food, and the roots of plants.

HERCULANEUM

DOMUS (TOWN HOUSE)

SKELETON FROM THE HARBOR

CARBONIZED WOODEN CUPBOARD

The neighboring town of Herculaneum was buried under up to 72 ft (22 m) of boiling mud, which flowed down the mountainside after the eruption. Many items were preserved here by carbonization—partial burning. These include furniture, the hull of a boat, cloth, and loaves of bread. The skeletons of 300 people have been found in the harbor, from where they were trying to escape. Because the mud was so deep, Herculaneum is much harder to excavate than Pompeii. Many of its secrets are still to be uncovered.

A ROMAN HOUSE

Thanks to the wonderful preservation of buildings in Pompeii, it is possible to see exactly what a wealthy Roman's house (*domus*) looked like, room by room. Although the house is empty and quiet now, in Roman times it would have been a bustling, noisy place. Every morning, visitors would file into the *atrium* (entrance hall), waiting to see the head of the household. Slaves ran errands, moving from room to room, while young children played with their toys and pets, and the women sat together spinning wool.

▲ BEWARE OF THE DOG
Houses were designed to be safe from thieves, so the few outside windows were small. Light came from internal courtyards. Also, the family often kept a fierce guard dog, and, as a warning, there might be a mosaic of a dog at the entrance with the words *Cave Canem* ("Beware of the Dog!")

▲ GARDENS
Wealthy Romans loved gardens, which were neatly laid out with hedges, paths, fountains, statues, and columns. Although the original plants were destroyed by the eruption, their roots left spaces in the earth providing clues to what the Romans liked to grow. Some of the gardens have been replanted, such as this colonnaded garden in nearby Herculaneum.

houses

▲ ATRIUM
The main entrance hall had an opening in the roof, known as the *compluvium*, through which light would flood in. Directly below was the *impluvium*, a shallow rectangular pool, often lined with marble, to gather rainwater. The *atrium* was the most public space in the house.

▲ TABLINUM
Behind the *atrium* was the *tablinum*, the head of the house's study, which would often look out onto the garden. Here the owner received clients, less-wealthy Romans who came to ask him for favors. In return for legal or financial help, clients gave their patrons political and social support. Important family documents were kept in a chest in the *tablinum*.

▲ TRICLINIUM
The *triclinium*, or dining room, was named after the three sloping couches where the diners reclined to eat. The platform would have been spread with comfortable cushions. Some houses had an outdoor *triclinium*, as shown here, where the family could enjoy eating outdoors on summer days, as well as a main dining area indoors.

STYLES OF WALL PAINTING

FALSE DOOR
Interior walls were decorated in a variety of styles. From 80 B.C.E., there was a fashion for adding architectural features, such as columns, windows, or doors, to trick the eye into believing they were real three-dimensional objects. Variations on this theme included open windows and doorways that looked out onto imaginary views.

RICH DECORATION
Over time, wall paintings, such as this one from the House of the Vettii, grew ever more elaborate. Figures are framed by delicate architectural features, a style that came into fashion shortly before Vesuvius erupted. The owners were two freedmen who had become wealthy businessmen, so the paintings were an expression of their new-found status.

LANDSCAPE
Walls were also painted with scenes from mythology and views of real landscapes. This beautiful painting, made with loose, free strokes, shows a busy harbor in the Bay of Naples. The scene includes columns topped with statues, boats, fishermen, and people waiting at the dock. The view would have been familiar to the people living in the house.

KITCHENS AND STORAGE

The kitchens in Pompeii were small and plain, for they would be seen only by the slaves who worked there. There was usually a raised brick oven, on top of which charcoal was burned. Kitchens were equipped with a wide range of utensils, including this strainer which would have been used for straining wine or sauces. Food supplies were stored in pots called *amphorae*, some of which would be buried in the ground to keep them cool.

BRONZE STRAINER

MUFFIN TIN

COOK'S KNIFE

▲ LARARIUM
Every house had a miniature shrine, called a *lararium*, where offerings were made to the gods who watched over the family and the home. This shrine has been made to resemble a small temple, with a painting of the goddess Minerva on the wall. Bronze statuettes of the household gods would have stood on the shelf.

▲ CALDARIUM
Although most Pompeiians were happy to visit the public baths, a few of the richest houses in Pompeii had their own private bath suites. These would include hot rooms with a hypocaust or underfloor heating, which would have been very expensive to run. This is the elaborately decorated *caldarium*, or hot room, of an imposing mansion known as the House of the Menander.

▲ FLORA AND FAUNA
The Pompeiians loved their gardens so much that they even had garden scenes, such as this one, painted on their walls to show a variety of birds and flowers. In the depths of winter, when their own gardens were mostly bare, these frescoes were a reminder that spring would come again.

FAMILY LIFE

The word "family" comes from the Latin *familia*. The head of a traditional Roman family was the oldest male, called the *paterfamilias* ("father of the family"). In theory, he had power of life or death over all the members of his family, which included his children and grandchildren. He chose husbands and wives for his sons and daughters, arranging their marriages with another *paterfamilias*. Adult sons became head of their own families only when the *paterfamilias* died. Daughters often remained under their father's authority, even after they married.

◄ FAMILY PORTRAITS

The *paterfamilias* continued to watch over his family after death. His wax death mask was kept in the house, along with those of earlier heads of the family, and these were carried through the streets during funeral processions. Portrait busts of previous heads of the family, such as the ones shown here, were also displayed. The purpose of such sculptures was to show off the family's earlier achievements and to inspire younger generations to live up to their ancestors.

Clasped hands, showing marriage as a partnership

◄ WEDDING RING

There was often a betrothal ceremony, when the groom gave the bride a ring, which she wore on the third finger of her left hand. According to the writer Aulus Gellius, this finger was chosen because "when the human body is cut open, a very delicate nerve is found which starts from this finger and travels to the heart".

▼ WEDDING CEREMONY

The bride wore a white dress and a flame-colored veil. Her husband-to-be carried her over the threshold of his house. This was to prevent her from stumbling, which would be an unlucky omen. The couple then swore oaths in front of witnesses to live together as husband and wife. June was the most popular month for weddings, because it was a time sacred to Juno, goddess of marriage. This is a 19th-century painting of a wedding held in the bridegroom's home.

Kithara, a type of lyre

Bride wears a veil and flowers in her hair

Groom carries fruit

Altar

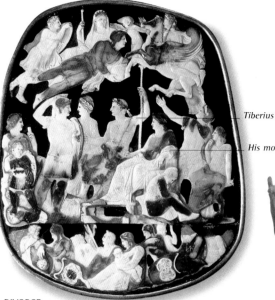

▲ DIVORCE

Divorce was common, particularly in the imperial family, where marriages were made and unmade for political reasons. In 12 B.C.E. Emperor Augustus ordered his stepson, Tiberius (shown in this cameo), to divorce his beloved wife, Vipsania. Augustus knew that Tiberius would succeed him as emperor, and wanted him to marry his daughter, Julia, so that his own descendants would later rule. Tiberius, who was forbidden from seeing Vipsania, was deeply unhappy in his new marriage to Julia.

Tiberius

His mother, Livia

Toga covers head

SHRINE FOR BUSTS AND MASKS OF ANCESTORS, POMPEII

BRONZE FIGURE OF A GENIUS

◄ HOUSEHOLD SHRINES

Rich families would often have two household shrines. One held the portrait busts and wax masks of dead ancestors, prominently displayed in the entrance hall. The more private *lararium* shrine held statuettes of the gods who protected the home, as well as a figure representing the *genius* – the spirit, or life force, of the *paterfamilias*. He was usually shown as a man in a *toga*, which covered his head, the dress worn for worship.

family life

Inscription reads "tribune officer of the Victorious Sixth Legion"

▲ HUSBAND AND WIFE

This tombstone, of Sextus Adgennius Macrinus and his wife Licinia Flavilla, shows the very different roles of Roman men and women. The inscription details the husband's varied career path, including posts as a military officer, magistrate, and priest. His wife, however, has had only one public role—as a *flaminica* (priestess in the imperial cult). She has probably spent most of her life at home, raising children. Yet their busts are the same size, which shows they were equal partners in their marriage.

CHILDREN

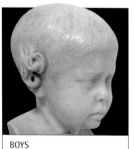

BOYS
The purpose of marriage was to have children, particularly boys, who would keep the family line going and bring in money when they married. The upper classes hoped for sons to increase the family's fame, by winning consulships, magistracies, and military commands.

GIRLS
Through marriage, girls could help make alliances with other influential families. Augustus married his daughter, Julia, to three different husbands for political reasons. Unlike boys, girls had to be provided with money, called a dowry, when they married.

CLOTHES AND FASHION

Roman men and women both wore a tunic as their basic item of clothing. This usually consisted of two rectangular pieces of woven woolen cloth joined at the shoulders. Members of the rich senatorial class wore a tunic with a broad purple stripe running down from the shoulder. A variety of cloaks or shawls were worn over the tunic, including the *palla* worn by rich women and the *toga* of Roman male citizens. The *toga* was so important to the Romans that the poet Vergil described his countrymen as "masters of the earth, the race that wears the *toga*."

◄ THE TOGA
This statue shows just how elaborate a *toga* could be. The large piece of semicircular woolen cloth was 18 ft (5.5 m) long and 9 ft (2.7 m) wide. It was draped over the left shoulder with one end reaching to the ground. The other end was then passed around the back and under the right arm and back over the left shoulder. The *toga* was expensive and needed frequent washing. It was also heavy and awkward to wear, but it made the wearer look dignified.

clothes

Palla

◄ WOMEN'S DRESS
This marble statue is of a rich Roman lady called Cornelia Antonia, who lived in the 2nd century C.E. Over a floor-length tunic she wears a *palla*, which she has draped over her head. The fabric for her clothes would have been brightly coloured. Her *palla* is so tightly wrapped around her that she cannot use her arms. Such impractical clothing was a sign of high status. It showed that she did not have to work for a living, and had slaves to dress her.

◄ DIFFERENT TOGAS
The central figure in this painting wears a *toga praetexta*, with a purple border to indicate his status. This was worn by magistrates and the sons of wealthy citizens before they came of age. For mourning, Romans wore a dark *toga pulla*, while for men campaigning for office there was a chalk-whitened *toga candida*. This is the origin of our word "candidate."

MEN'S HAIRSTYLES

STYLE LEADERS
Emperors, whose portraits appeared on every coin, led the way in new hairstyles. People copied the emperor as a way of showing loyalty, or simply to be up-to-date. Emperor Nero, who ruled 54–68 C.E., grew his hair long at the back and had sideburns that met under his chin—a style he copied from charioteers. This look went out of fashion when Nero was overthrown.

BEARDS
Romans were clean-shaven until Hadrian came to the throne in 117 C.E. He had grown a beard, partly to show his admiration for the famous Greeks of an earlier age, who were all bearded. He may also have wanted to hide a scar on his chin. Beards quickly became the fashion again. Roman razors were poor quality, so it was a relief not to have to visit the barber every morning.

CLEAN-SHAVEN
Beards remained popular until the early 4th century C.E., when Rome once more had a clean-shaven emperor—Constantine. By shaving, Constantine probably hoped to remind people of the greatest Roman emperors of an earlier age, such as Augustus and Trajan, the warrior emperor. Like Trajan, Constantine also combed his hair forward.

◄ GETTING DRESSED

This wall painting from Herculaneum shows a lady helping a girl, perhaps her daughter, with her hair. In reality, this would be done by slaves, and the richest ladies might have several slaves helping them dress each morning. One slave would hold up a mirror of polished metal in front of her mistress, while her skilled *ornatrix* (hairdresser and cosmetics slave), would pluck her eyebrows, apply cosmetics, and arrange her hair, often using heated curling tongs. Meanwhile, other slaves might manicure the lady's fingernails, and dab her with perfume.

Gold earring in the form of a dolphin

Bone hairpin with the bust of a woman with an elaborate hairstyle

Gold necklace

Yellow bead from a necklace

JEWELRY ►

Rich Roman women wore a vast amount of jewelry, including precious stones, such as emeralds, rubies, and pearls imported from India, and amber from the Baltic, far to the north. Women were often buried with their favorite ornaments, and because gold and precious stones do not decay in the ground, many pieces of Roman jewelry survive today. Most of the items shown here come from women's graves.

Ring carved with a relief, which was pressed into wax to seal documents

Flavian hairstyle with an abundance of ringlets

◄ COSMETICS

This lovely coffin portrait is a "mummy mask" from Roman Egypt, dating from the late 2nd century C.E. The lady represents the Roman ideal of beauty, with her pale pink-tinted skin, red lips, and dark eyebrows and lashes. She looks as if she is not wearing makeup, yet Roman women used a wide variety of cosmetics to create this effect. They had wine dregs for reddening lips and cheeks, chalk or lead for white foundation, and soot for eyeliner. These were all mixed with a base cream made from animal fat.

▲ WOMEN'S HAIRSTYLES

The most elaborate hairstyles for Roman women were those worn under the Flavian family of emperors, who ruled from 69–138 C.E. Flavian ladies wore their hair in curls piled high on the head. Such hairstyles were often wigs, using blonde hair from German slave girls, and black hair imported from the East.

CHILDREN

We know a great deal about children's lives in Roman times from the mass of evidence that exists. There are portraits of boys and girls, toys from children's graves, and mosaics and reliefs showing children at play and going to school. Romans often talk affectionately about children in their letters. In the 2nd century C.E., for example, a man named Marcus Cornelius Fronto sent a letter to his son-in-law, describing his grandson, little Fronto, who was staying with him: "The one word your little Fronto continually says is 'da!' (Give!). I hand over whatever I can ... He shows signs of his grandfather's character too: he is particularly greedy for grapes."

▲ GROWING UP

The sarcophagus (stone coffin) of Marcus Cornelius Statius shows the stages in the life of a boy from a wealthy Roman family. On the left, the baby boy is being suckled by his mother, while her husband proudly looks on. In the center, watched by his father, the boy, now grown older, rides a toy chariot pulled by a ram. On the right, he recites his lessons to his father. In reality, the boy's upbringing would have been overseen by slaves, who have been left off the carving. Many babies were suckled by hired nurses rather than by their mothers, and Greek slaves often served as tutors in the homes of wealthy Romans.

Pupil reads from a papyrus scroll

Grammaticus

School chairs with high backs

Late pupil anxiously greets his teacher

▲ SCHOOL

Formal schooling was usually reserved for boys, who went through three stages of education. They were first taught to read and write by a *litterator*. The next stage was to study with a *grammaticus*, who introduced his pupils to literature, particularly the work of Greek writers. In their late teens, they went on to learn the skills of public speaking, taught by a *rhetor*. Classes were usually small, taking place in the master's home. This carved relief shows a *grammaticus* with a class of three boys. One of them has arrived late for his lesson.

children

◄ GIRLS

Roman girls were usually educated at home, though not always in their own home. Many were sent by their parents to live with friends or relatives, where they would be taught alongside other girls of their own age. They learned to read and write, to spin and weave, and to play musical instruments. They also had to learn to keep accounts because, as wives, they would be expected to run a household. When it was time to marry, they left their dolls as an offering to the gods at the household shrine. This ivory doll, which would once have had clothes, has a hairstyle made fashionable by Julia Domna, wife of Emperor Septimius Severus (ruled 193-211 C.E.).

Gold necklace

Hinged arm

COLORED GLASS
MARBLES

GLADIATOR DOLL

AGATE DICE

PULL-ALONG
TOY HORSE

CHILDREN'S GAMES

THE BRONZE FLY

For centuries, children have played versions of Blindman's Buff—shown in this 1559 painting by the Flemish artist, Pieter Brueghel. The Roman name for the game was "the bronze fly." The blindfolded child was spun around, while calling out "I will chase the bronze fly!" The others replied, "You will chase him but you won't catch him!"

BALL GAMES

Children played with balls made from wood or leather, which were stuffed with feathers or horsehair. Such balls did not bounce, so games involved throwing and catching. This wall painting from a tomb shows two young men throwing a ball. In another game, called *trigon*, three players stood in a triangle, throwing balls to each other.

KNUCKLEBONES

Games were played with the knucklebones (*tali*) of sheep or pigs. For a game, players took turns to throw the knucklebones in the air. They would then attempt to catch as many as possible on the backs of their hands. As this pottery model shows, this game was especially popular with girls and young women.

PLAYING WITH NUTS

One way of saying that someone was no longer a child was that they had "stopped playing with nuts." Nuts were thrown like marbles, as in this relief from Ostia. They were also used in a game called *par impar* ("odd or even"). One child held some nuts in a closed fist while another had to guess if their number was odd or even.

▲ TOYS

Finds from children's graves show that Roman children and today's boys and girls played with many of the same toys, including marbles, dolls, and pull-along animals. Boys had their own gladiator and soldier dolls. Children and adults both played at dice, made from bone or stone such as agate. People have been playing with dice for more than 3,000 years.

PETS ►

This mosaic shows a boy riding a toy chariot pulled by two peacocks. Although the scene is fantasy, Roman children did love birds, and kept them as pets. Among the most popular were starlings, ravens, magpies, and crows. Dogs were the commonest pets, while cats were introduced to Rome from Egypt in the 1st century C.E. Some families also kept pet monkeys, which they would teach to do tricks.

A DINNER PARTY

Rich Romans ate their main meal, called *cena*, in the evening, reclining on couches. For the host, this was a chance to display his wealth and taste, impressing guests with lavish dishes, unusual ingredients, and expensive tableware. A dinner party was like a theatrical performance, with the courses brought out in turn like new acts in a show. As the slaves came in carrying each course, the guests would gasp with admiration and astonishment, and might even show their appreciation with a round of applause.

Ornamental pool with fountain

Three couches were arranged around the side

Mosaic of Neptune and Amphitrite

OUTDOOR TRICLINIUM IN HERCULANEUM

◄ TRICLINIUM

Romans dined in the *triclinium*, reclining on three couches, which were covered with a mattress and cushions. The couches were arranged around a rectangular space, where a small table stood. The perfect number of diners was nine, with three to each couch. Guests were placed according to their social status, and the most important guests would recline on the central couch.

Couch holds just one person

SLAVES

Guests were greeted by slaves who washed and dried their feet, and then showed them to the *triclinium*. Slaves also cooked and served the meal, and carried water jugs and towels, so that the diners could wash their hands between courses. After the meal, the slaves would be able to eat the leftovers. This stone relief gives us a rare glimpse behind the scenes at a Roman banquet, where two slaves are pouring out the wine.

Pet dog begs for food

◄ VITELLIUS

Nobody loved food more than Emperor Vitellius, who ruled Rome for ten months in 69 C.E. Vitellius had an enormous appetite and ate three or four huge meals a day, a feat possible only because he made himself vomit in between. As emperor, he spent a great deal of money on food, sending naval ships to fetch exotic ingredients from distant lands. The most famous dish served to him had food arranged to look like the shield of the goddess Minerva, complete with the head of Medusa, a monster with snakes for hair. Among its many ingredients, brought to Rome from places as far apart as Spain and Syria, were flamingo tongues, pike livers, and the brains of pheasants and peacocks.

dinner parties

▲ FOOD
A typical banquet might consist of up to seven courses, including fish, meat, and poultry served with sauces. For dessert there was fresh fruit, nuts, and honey cake. A Roman cook book, written by Apicius, describes some of the lavish dishes on offer, including a recipe for squid stuffed with calf's brains seasoned with fennel.

▲ WINE
The Romans served wine in various ways—warmed, spiced, sweetened with honey, or cooled with snow. Honeyed wine (*mulsum*) was usually served at the start of the meal. Then stronger wine was mixed with water in a big bowl, and served in cups. The best-quality wine was thought to be Falernian, a white wine from southern Italy, which improved with age and might be kept for up to 20 years.

▲ ENTERTAINMENT
The host of a dinner party would also provide entertainment for his guests. This often took the form of music, played by a slave on a lyre, an instrument with strings that were plucked like a harp. Other slaves danced, performed acrobatics, juggled, gave readings from books, and did bird impressions.

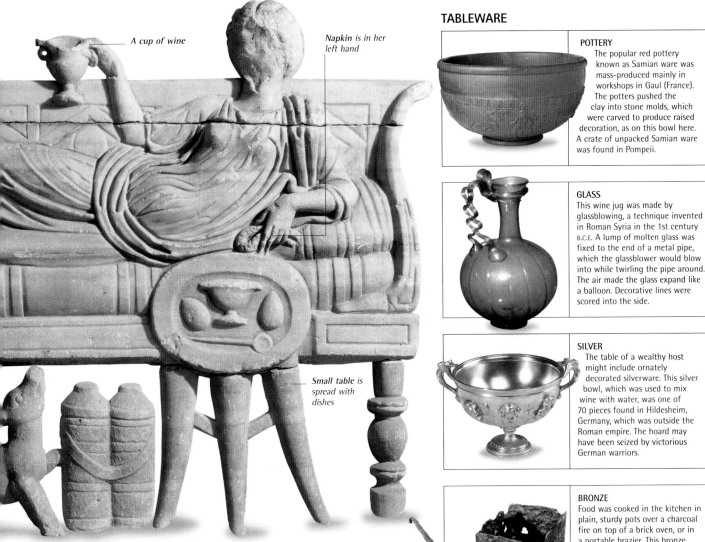

A cup of wine

Napkin is in her left hand

Small table is spread with dishes

▲ DINING RECLINING
Guests reclined on couches, like this lady on a tomb carving. They leaned on their left elbows while eating with their right hands, using a spoon and knife or their fingers—the fork had not yet been invented. Reclining was both comfortable and a sign of elegance, because poorer Romans did not lie down to eat. Guests spread napkins in front of them to protect the couch, and also to collect tidbits to take home with them.

TABLEWARE

POTTERY
The popular red pottery known as Samian ware was mass-produced mainly in workshops in Gaul (France). The potters pushed the clay into stone molds, which were carved to produce raised decoration, as on this bowl here. A crate of unpacked Samian ware was found in Pompeii.

GLASS
This wine jug was made by glassblowing, a technique invented in Roman Syria in the 1st century B.C.E. A lump of molten glass was fixed to the end of a metal pipe, which the glassblower would blow into while twirling the pipe around. The air made the glass expand like a balloon. Decorative lines were scored into the side.

SILVER
The table of a wealthy host might include ornately decorated silverware. This silver bowl, which was used to mix wine with water, was one of 70 pieces found in Hildesheim, Germany, which was outside the Roman empire. The hoard may have been seized by victorious German warriors.

BRONZE
Food was cooked in the kitchen in plain, sturdy pots over a charcoal fire on top of a brick oven, or in a portable brazier. This bronze brazier might also have been carried through to the *triclinium* and used to keep dishes warm. Both the brazier and the serving spoon were found at a Roman site in northern France.

DEATH

The Romans had various ideas of what would happen to them after death. From the Greeks, they took the belief that a dead person's spirit was rowed across a mythical river to a dark underworld. So the dead were buried with a coin in their mouths as a fee for the ferryman who would take them. There was also the belief that the dead remained in or around their tombs, where they could receive offerings. Whatever their belief, everyone felt that it was important to be given a proper funeral and a grave marker of some kind, so they would not be forgotten.

▲ BURIAL SOCIETY
People who could not afford to pay for their own tomb might join a burial society, and pay for a place in a communal one called a *columbarium* ("pigeon house"). Members of burial societies held annual feasts, so they could get to know their companions in the afterlife. Each of these niches once held an urn, containing the ashes of a dead Roman.

▲ BURIAL
In early times in the western half of the empire, the dead were cremated, while in the east the custom was to bury the body whole. In Emesa (modern Homs) in Syria, the wealthy were buried wearing beautiful gold masks such as this one. In the 2nd century C.E., the practice of burial (inhumation) gradually spread westward.

◄ ROADSIDE TOMBS
The dead were usually taken to tombs lining the main road outside a town. This was partly so that their spirits were at a safe distance and could not haunt the living. The road was also a good place for a family to display their wealth and status with an impressive tomb.

Ashes of the dead were buried beneath each jar

DRINKS FOR THE DEAD ▲

On special occasions, such as festivals for the dead and on the birthday of the deceased, families would visit the tomb and share a meal with departed loved ones. Sunken jars (*amphorae*), such as these from Ostia, near Rome, were used to pour wine into the underworld. The jars served as the grave markers of people who could not afford carved memorials.

TOMB CARVINGS

PHYSICIAN
Tomb carvings often show the departed doing the work they did in life. This carving shows an oculist, a physician specializing in eye diseases. He carefully applies ointment to the patient's eye from the pot he is holding. The patient sits on a raised chair, allowing the oculist to look into his eyes without bending.

MIDWIFE
This relief comes from the tomb of a midwife, a woman who helps at a birth. In Roman times mothers gave birth while sitting on a chair. The midwife prepares to deliver the baby, while another woman holds the mother-to-be from behind. Inscriptions on other tombstones show that many women died during childbirth.

STOREKEEPER
The life of a storekeeper is commemorated in this relief on a tomb in Ostia. This is not a specific portrait of the dead man, however, for almost exactly the same scene appears on numerous tomb carvings. His family would simply have bought a relief of a store scene from a sculptor specializing in tomb carvings.

BAKER
Here a baker is pushing bread into an oven, which would have been at the back of the bakery. The relief comes from a huge tomb in Rome belonging to a rich baker called Marcus Vergilius Eurysaces. The man in this carving is not Eurysaces himself, however, but one of the many slaves who worked in his bakery.

◄ DI MANES
Roman cemeteries contain not only tombs, but also altars to the dead, where offerings were made. The Romans thought of the dead as belonging to a body of gods or spirits, called the *di manes* (spirits of the dead). These were honored during three festivals, *Feralia* and *Parentalia*, when family members visited their graves, and *Lemuria*, when offerings were made to wandering ghosts—those who had not had proper burials.

Tomb altar from the late 1st century C.E., dedicated to "a very dear wife"

CHILDREN ►
In this carving on a tombstone found in France, a father holds the hand of his dead daughter. The death of children like this little girl was a common event in Roman times, because there were many illnesses for which cures had not been found. The writer Martial wrote a poem in memory of a favorite slave girl called Erotion, who died when she was only six. It ends, "Don't let the turf lie hard on her tender bones—and earth, don't be heavy on her, for she was no great weight on you."

Chains tie slaves together

A SLAVE'S TAG COLLAR

Name and address of slave's owner

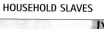

◄ ON SALE
The relief on the left, from Miletus in Asia Minor, shows three slaves on sale in a market. They are almost naked, so that buyers could see how fit and strong they were. Slaves would often carry a sign, on which was written their age and nationality, and any special skills, health problems, or bad habits. Buyers would inspect each slave closely, feeling his muscles and inspecting his teeth, just as they would a horse. Once sold, the slave might be branded or forced to wear a bronze identity tag, in case he ran away. There were professional slavecatchers, called *fugitivarii*, whose job was to hunt down runaway slaves.

SLAVES

The word "servant" comes from the Latin *servus*, meaning a slave—someone owned by another person as property. Conditions of slavery varied greatly, from the comfortable lives of many household slaves, to the harsh existence of the underfed and overworked slaves in mines and quarries and on farming estates. Like most ancient peoples, the Romans took slavery for granted. Yet many writers argued that slaves should be well treated. The philosopher Seneca declared, "They may be slaves but they are also men—men with whom we share the same roof, our humble friends."

HOUSEHOLD SLAVES

Household slaves of rich owners often had a better life than the free poor, and they could even own slaves themselves. One day a year, during the festival of *Saturnalia*, many were even allowed to give orders to their masters. Those brought up in their owners' homes from early childhood were seen as members of the family. This mosaic shows a slave boy, called Junius, working in the kitchen. His owners must have been very fond of him to pay to have his portrait made.

Chain is attached to metal collar

Pants indicate these are northern barbarians

Guard holds chain

◄ A SUPPLY OF SLAVES
This pottery relief shows two prisoners of war being led through Rome in a triumphal procession. Warfare was an important source of slaves during the early years of the empire, when it was still expanding. Slaves were also bred from other slaves, or brought in from lands outside the empire by foreign slave dealers. The biggest market was on the tiny Greek island of Delos, which offered slaves with specialist skills, such as cooks, doctors, teachers, and musicians. People could also be sentenced to slavery for crimes and forced to do hard labor. They would often be kept in chains, and were locked away at night in a prison called an *ergastulum*.

GAINING FREEDOM ▶

Many Romans gave their slaves a reason to work hard by paying them wages. Slaves could save this money to buy their own freedom, which might also be given as a reward for loyal service. There was a special freeing (manumission) ceremony, performed before a magistrate, where the owner struck the slave, who wore a tall felt cap. The blow represented the slave's last indignity, and protection from being struck in future. Freed slaves (freedmen) were often set up in business by their former owners, becoming slave owners in their own right.

Liberty cap

Owner

Whip

Slave kneels to be struck

KIRK DOUGLAS AS SPARTACUS

slaves

▲ FROM SLAVE TO EMPEROR

Although freed slaves could not be magistrates, their children could reach the highest positions in society. The most striking example is Pertinax, the son of a freed slave, who rose through the ranks of the Roman army, eventually becoming consul, and then emperor of Rome in 192–3 C.E.

SLAVE KING ▲

In Sicily, in the 2nd century B.C.E., there was a vast number of Greek-speaking slaves following Rome's conquest of the east. Around 135 B.C.E., the badly treated slaves rose in rebellion, led by a Syrian slave called Eunus, who was declared king. Eunus created a miniature version of the Seleucid kingdom (the state which included his Syrian homeland), which he ruled from the mountain stronghold at Enna in central Sicily. He took the name Antiochus, common among Seleucids, wore a crown, and minted coins bearing his head. After the rebellion was crushed in 131 B.C.E., he was found hiding in a cave with his bath attendant and jester. He later died in prison.

◀ SPARTACUS

The 1960 movie *Spartacus* is based on the true story of the gladiator who led the last great slave rebellion, in 73–1 B.C.E. With his fellow gladiators, he broke out of his barracks in Capua, in southern Italy, and raised an army. Slaves, along with many free poor people, rushed to join him. After three years roaming Italy, during which he defeated several Roman armies, Spartacus tried but failed to cross over to Sicily. He then lost his final battle, in which he was probably killed. Around 6,000 of his followers were crucified.

THE ARMY OF TRAJAN

The Roman empire reached its greatest extent under Emperor Trajan, who ruled from 98–117 C.E. He was a great general, who spent most of his life with the army, spreading Roman rule north of the Danube and as far east as Iraq. After his death, Trajan's ashes were placed in the base of a marble column carved with reliefs of his campaigns in Dacia (Romania). There are around 2,600 figures on the column, shown in such detail that it is even possible to make out shield decorations. It shows how Roman soldiers marched, crossed rivers, built camps, foraged for food, and fought and won their battles.

Column is hollow, with a spiral staircase inside, leading to a viewing platform

◀ TRAJAN
Before he became emperor, Trajan was Rome's leading general, commanding the armies in Germany. He was so successful and popular with his soldiers that the previous emperor, Nerva, decided to adopt him as his heir. As emperor, he fought two campaigns in Dacia, amassing great wealth, which he used to build a grand new forum in Rome. This statue shows him dressed as a Roman general addressing his troops.

Trajan's army

TRAJAN'S COLUMN ▲
The column, which is 125 ft (38 m) high, was made from 20 drums of white Italian marble, placed on top of each other. Then the scenes were carved, from the bottom upward, by sculptors standing on scaffolding. At the top was a gilded statue of Trajan, looking down on the forum he created. The column is a monument both to Trajan and to his soldiers, who are shown climbing up around the sides in a continuous spiral frieze.

Iron helmet, with bronze decoration

◄ ROMAN LEGIONARY

The finest soldiers in Trajan's army were heavily armed legionaries, all Roman citizens. They wore armor made of thin iron plates that overlapped, allowing them to bend and move freely. Each legionary carried two javelins, for throwing, and a short sword for stabbing at close quarters. The javelins had long iron heads that bent on impact. If one stuck in an enemy's shield, he would find it hard to pull out, and impossible to throw back.

Spear, a thrusting weapon used by Roman cavalrymen

Javelin with a long iron head, called a pilum

Woolen tunic dyed red

Armour of metal strips held together with leather strips on the inside

Gladius, a short sword with a wooden handle

Cingulum, a belt with an apron of leather strips studded with metal

Scabbard for sword, worn on the right side

▲ AUXILIARIES

Fighting alongside the legionaries were non-citizen soldiers, called auxiliaries. They were lightly armed and fought in specialized ways, such as with slings and bows. As a reward for service, auxiliaries were given Roman citizenship when they retired. These archers, with short bows and long tunics, may be from Syria or Arabia.

Standard was carried by a signifer wearing a bearskin

Centurion with horizontal crest

Long, curved wooden shields, painted with thunderbolts, eagle wings, and garlands

CENTURY ►

In Trajan's time, there were 30 Roman legions, each with around 5,500 men. A legion was split into ten divisions, called cohorts, in turn divided into smaller units, called centuries. Here is a typical century, made up of 80 legionaries and commanded by an officer called a centurion, who wears a horizontal crest on his helmet and greaves (shin guards).

THE CONQUERING ARMY (SCENES FROM TRAJAN'S COLUMN)

SACRIFICING
Before any important undertaking, such as crossing a river or attacking a fort, the Roman army sacrificed animals to the gods. In this scene, a pig is being led in a sacrificial procession into a fort.

BUILDING
The column shows the soldiers building temporary marching camps and permanent stone forts, as in this scene. Construction was made easier because camps and forts followed a standard plan.

FIGHTING
Legionaries were trained to use different tactics in response to various trumpet signals. These soldiers attacking a fort have put their shields above their heads, in a formation called a *testudo*, or tortoise.

LEADING
Trajan appears in many scenes on the column—receiving and sending messages, making rousing speeches to his men, and awarding prizes for bravery. Here he oversees a sacrifice in his role as priest.

FOLLOWING
Standards were holy objects that soldiers followed into battle. Each legion had a standard with Jupiter's eagle on top, as well as another with the emblem of their particular legion—in this case a ram.

▲ HADRIAN'S WALL

Local limestone

The wall is still an impressive structure today, but in Roman times it was more than 15 ft (4.5 m) high. Every Roman mile (4,852 ft/1,479 m) there was a milecastle, or small stone fort, each holding a few dozen soldiers. Between each milecastle there were two small lookout turrets. As this picture shows, the wall followed high ground wherever possible, making it even harder to attack. On flat ground, deep ditches running on each side of the wall provided further defense against attackers.

ON THE FRONTIERS

Hadrian, who succeeded Trajan as emperor in 117 C.E., believed that the empire had grown too large to be properly defended. He gave up some of Trajan's conquests and built more lasting defenses along the new frontiers. In Europe, these followed the great rivers, the Rhine and the Danube, where he built new forts and watchtowers. He also built a great wall running for 73 miles (117 km) across northern Britain. It protected the empire from the warlike tribes to the north and controlled the movement of people living on either side. The wall also acted as a visible reminder of Rome's power.

fortifications

◄ HADRIAN

This is a bronze head from a statue of Emperor Hadrian, who ruled from 117 C.E. until 138 C.E. A highly intelligent and hard-working ruler, Hadrian refused to conquer new territory, concentrating instead on strengthening the frontiers. This new policy risked offending the army, which depended on war to win booty and glory. Hadrian spent much of his reign visiting frontier forts, winning over his soldiers. Hadrian's Wall was built following his visit to Britain in 122 C.E.

THE NEW FRONTIERS

This map shows the empire under Hadrian, with its fortified frontiers (limes) shown here in red. At the top, Hadrian's Wall crosses Britain at its narrowest point. Other frontiers are provided by natural boundaries, such as the rivers of Europe and the North African desert.

FORTS ►

This is Housesteads, one of 15 large forts built along the wall. Roman forts followed a standard plan, with four main entrances and a central headquarters building next to the commanding officer's house. Around these buildings were a hospital, granaries, and barrack blocks. Outside the fort there was a civilian settlement, called a *vicus*. Traders settled here, opening shops and bars, where the soldiers relaxed when off duty.

PARTS OF A ROMAN FORT

Key to fort	
1. West Gate	5. Granary
2. Hospital	6. Barracks
3. Headquarters	7. Latrines
4. Commander's house	8. *Vicus*

SHRINE AND STRONGROOM

The most important part of a fort's headquarters was the shrine. Here the standards stood beside a statue of the emperor. Both were regarded as sacred objects, and were offered sacrifices. The money to pay the soldiers' wages and other valuables were kept in a strongroom beneath the shrine.

GRANARY

Grain for the soldiers' bread was stored in a granary. The grain was provided by local farmers as a tax. Granaries can be recognized by rows of stone columns, shown in the background here, which supported a raised floor. Air circulating beneath the floor kept the grain dry and stopped it from turning moldy.

BATH AND TOILET

Roman soldiers expected to be provided with bathhouses. These were usually outside the walls. (Furnaces used to heat the bath water were a fire risk.) The changing room for this bathhouse can be seen in the background. In the foreground is the communal latrine, with a drain to flush away toilet waste.

Regina sits in a wicker chair, mending clothes

LETTERS FROM THE WALL ►

At Vindolanda, another fort on Hadrian's Wall, archaeologists have unearthed more than 1,000 thin, wooden writing tablets, preserved by the waterlogged soil. These include private letters, shopping lists, and official reports. This letter is an invitation to a birthday party, which an officer's wife called Claudia Severa sent to Sulpicia Lepidina, wife of the commander at Vindolanda. Most of it was written by a secretary, but Claudia added at the end, in her own handwriting, "I shall expect you sister. Farewell sister, my dearest soul."

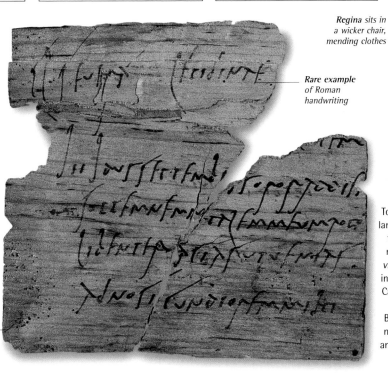

Rare example of Roman handwriting

Wooden tablet, about the size of a modern postcard

REGINA ▲

Tombstones reveal that people from many lands lived along Hadrian's Wall. This is the tombstone of Regina—whose Latin name means queen—a woman who lived in the *vicus* by the fort in Arbeia (South Shields, in northern England). She belonged to the Catuvellauni tribe, whose homeland lay in southern Britain. Regina was married to Barates, a trader from Palmyra, in what is now Syria. The inscription is in both Latin and Palmyrene. Regina would have spoken a British language, too.

ROMAN ROADS

The Romans constructed a network of long, straight roads with deep foundations. Unlike earlier trackways, which turned into squelchy mud under heavy rain, Roman roads were well drained and could be used in all weathers. Good roads were needed throughout the empire so that armies and official messengers could travel quickly from place to place. Yet they benefited everyone, from traders and farmers bringing goods to market by oxcart, to sick people traveling to healing shrines.

Originally graveled, the paving was added from 295 B.C.E.

BUILDING A ROAD

PLANNING
The Romans planned their roads to be as straight as possible, even if this meant climbing steep hills. As conquerors they could build on anyone's land without asking permission, so they chose the most direct route between two places. Roman surveyors took sightings using beacons—fires on hilltops. This is an aerial view of a section of Watling Street, one of the major Roman roads in Britain. In places the ancient road is still in use today.

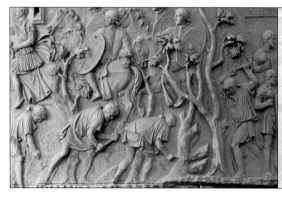

PREPARATION
This scene from Trajan's column shows the next stage in building a road. These soldiers are clearing land by chopping down trees. Once they had done this, they would dig a wide trench, several metres deep, for the road itself, and two smaller trenches alongside it for drainage. The wide trench would then be packed with whatever materials were available locally. This back-breaking work might also be done by slaves or prisoners of war.

ROAD LAYERS
For the lowest level of the road, the Romans laid down large stones or rubble to aid drainage. On top of this, there was a middle layer of finer material, such as gravel and sand, which was firmly packed down. Then a hard surface, called "metaling," was laid down. This was usually gravel, but sometimes paving stones or iron slag (waste from iron-making) were used. This paved road in Yorkshire, England, is unusual in having a central drainage gutter.

▼ THE APPIAN WAY

The first major Roman road to be built was the Appian Way. Begun in 312 B.C.E., the road went south from Rome to Capua. It was later extended until it stretched for 232 miles (374 km), to Brundisium (modern Brindisi), the port in the heel of Italy.

Roman roads

BRIDGES ►

The roadbuilders spanned rivers and deep gorges with arched bridges. One of the longest is this bridge crossing the Guadiana River in Mérida, southwest Spain, built in the 1st century C.E. Still used as a footbridge today, it has 64 granite arches and is a mighty 2,575 ft (785 m) long.

▲ MESSENGERS

Horseriders carried official messages by relay along the roads, stopping for fresh horses at lodging houses situated at regular intervals along the route. Messages would usually be carried at a rate of 50 miles (80 km) a day—though riders would travel much faster if the news was urgent. In 69 C.E., when the armies in Germany rebelled against Emperor Galba, the news traveled to him in Rome at a rate of 150 miles (240 km) a day.

TRAVEL GUIDES

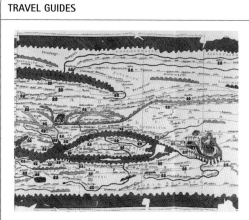

Roman travelers could consult guidebooks and road maps. This is a 13th-century copy of a Roman road map, showing major towns and the distances between them. This section shows part of the Middle East, with the island of Cyprus in the center. The seas are the wrong shape, but that did not matter, because this was designed for land travelers. More information came from milestones—pillars set up at intervals along the roads. These milestones were inscribed with the distance to the nearest town, as well as the name of the emperor who had built or repaired the stretch of road.

MILESTONE

TRAVELING EMPEROR ►

Emperor Hadrian was a great traveler, who spent much of his reign on the move with his court. He traveled in order to strengthen the frontiers of his empire and reform the government of the provinces. He was also curious to see different lands. Outside Rome, he built a huge palace in Tibur (Tivoli), with copies of many of the buildings he had seen on his travels. This pool, surrounded by columns and statues, is based on a famous Egyptian canal linking Alexandria with the town of Canopus.

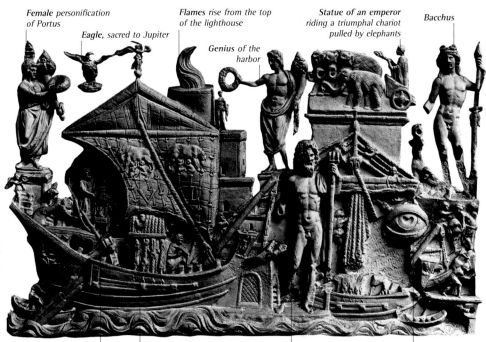

The map shows trade routes and goods across the Roman Empire and surrounding regions.

Amber · Amber · Slaves · Lead · Gold · Iron · Tin · Dover · Gesoriacum · Animal Hides Slaves · Textiles · Glass · Pottery · Silver · Iron · Iron · Gold · Iron · Black Sea · Aral Sea · Caspian Sea · Brigantium · Textiles · Silver · Silver · Gold · Byzantium · Precious Stones · Gold · Lead · Massilia · Corsica · Ostia · Rome · Olive Oil · Tin · Copper · ROMAN EMPIRE · Antioch · Sardinia · Sicily · Wine · Silver · PARTHIAN EMPIRE · Euphrates · Tigris · Babylon · Gades · Carthage · Olive Oil · Grain · Crete · Cyprus · Timber · Tyre · Timber · Jerusalem · Petra · Charax · Tingis · Timber · Grain · Mediterranean Sea · Gerra · Asabon · Russadir · Timber · Grain · Cyrene · Alexandria · Glass Grain Textiles Papyrus · Wine · Ommana · ARABIA · Myos Hormus · Nile · Berenice · Gold · MEROITIC EMPIRE · Red Sea · Tortoiseshell Spices Precious Stones Slaves · Zenobia · Gold · Meroe · Adulis · Incense · Cana · KINGDOM OF AKSUM · Aden · Animals Ivory Slaves · Avalites · Emporion

ROUTES INTO ROME

Via Clodia · Caere · Veii · Via Salaria · Nomentum · Via Aurelia · ROME · Via Tiburtina · Anio · Alsium · Fregenae · Gabii · Via Portuensis · Tiber · Via Appia · Portus · Ostia · Via Ostiensis · Bovillae · Aricia · Tyrrhenian Sea · Lavinium

TRADE

Roman rule provided peace, known as *Pax Romana* ("Roman peace"), to all the lands around the Mediterranean Sea. The Roman navy hunted down pirates, which helped trade flourish. It was now much safer for merchants to sail without fear of attack. The rich empire was also a market for goods from distant lands, such as China (silk), India (spices), and the Baltic (amber). In the 2nd century AD, the Greek writer, Aelius Aristides, marveled at the goods available in Rome: "One can see cargoes from India and southern Arabia in such numbers that one must conclude that the trees in those lands have been stripped bare."

◄ NEW PORTS
Roman emperors encouraged trade by building new harbors. This coin, issued by Emperor Nero in 64 C.E., celebrates the completion of a new harbor for Rome, called Portus. The existing harbor at nearby Ostia was too shallow for the largest ships to enter, so their goods had to be transferred to smaller vessels to be brought ashore. The coin shows the harbor crowded with merchant ships. The flames of the lighthouse can be seen at the top.

SAFE ARRIVAL IN PORTUS ►
A carved relief from Portus shows the arrival of two merchant ships carrying wine. While the ship on the right is already being unloaded, the second sails in, passing the tall lighthouse. The ship is powered by a single square sail, and steered by a pair of oars at the stern (rear). On the deck, sailors are sacrificing to the gods, thanking them for another safe journey. The relief was commissioned by a wine merchant to honor Neptune, god of the sea, and Bacchus, god of wine.

Female personification of Portus

Eagle, sacred to Jupiter

Flames rise from the top of the lighthouse

Genius of the harbor

Statue of an emperor riding a triumphal chariot pulled by elephants

Bacchus

Sacrifice offered to the gods

Sail with images of the she-wolf nursing Romulus and Remus

Neptune

Eye, thought to protect from evil

◀ TRADE ROUTES

Trade routes across Europe and Asia allowed the Romans to buy goods from faraway lands, such as China and India. Spices, particularly Indian pepper, were in huge demand in the Roman Empire. Pepper was even added to sweet dishes. The Chinese also bought Roman goods, such as Syrian glass, which has been found in Chinese tombs.

trade

KUSHAN EMPIRE

Horses

Himalayas

Silk Road

Chang'an Luoyang

Incense Silk Clothing

Hangzhou

East China Sea

HAN EMPIRE OF CHINA Fuzhou

Barbaricon

INDIA

Barygaza

Manidagora

Arabian Sea

Cattigara

Precious Stones Clothing Timber Tortoiseshell Ivory Spices Incense

Bay of Bengal

Thaton

Ivory Timber Spices

Oc Eo

Muziris

INDIAN OCEAN

Trang

Vessel of burning charcoal

WIND GOD ▲

Ships with large, square sails were effective only when the wind was behind them. Seafarers had to wait for the wind to be blowing in the right direction before setting off. Books of sailing directions did not say, "sail northwest," but, "sail with such-and-such a wind." Each wind was thought to have its own personality and was regarded as a god. Sailors would pray to a particular wind god, asking him to blow for them. This relief detail shows Skiron, the northwestern wind—hot and dry in summer, but cold in winter.

COINS

Trade was boosted by the creation of a standard coinage, used across the empire and even beyond. This gold *aureus* was the most valuable coin of all. One *aureus* was worth 25 silver coins called *denarii*, 100 mixed metal coins called *sestertii*, or 400 bronze coins called *dupondii*. Roman coins were originally minted in the Temple of Juno Moneta in Rome, the origin of the word "money."

Top half was added centuries later

◀ LIGHTHOUSES

Tall lighthouses, such as this ruined one in Dover, in England (far left), served as landmarks for sailors. Bonfires would be lit on top of them at night. For hundreds of years, a fire on top of this tower guided Roman ships across the Channel, and safely into harbor. Lighthouses also symbolized the supposed power of the emperor over the sea.

Anglo-Saxon church

Roman walls of flint and stone

FARMING

Although town life was important to the Romans, throughout the empire most people lived in the countryside, farming the land. There were farms of all sizes, from small farms worked by peasants to vast estates owned by the rich but worked by slaves. Upper-class Romans were landowners who, like aristocrats throughout history, saw farming as the most honourable source of wealth. Buying land, to be passed down through the family line, was a more secure investment than trade. Country estates also enabled wealthy Romans to indulge their passion for hunting. The rich would often own both a townhouse, called a *domus*, and a large country house, called a *villa*.

Ornamental pool

Colonnaded walkway

Farm buildings

Villa

Mars in full armor

Well

Donkey

Geese

Sunken storage pots

▲ VILLAS
Hundreds of Roman *villas* have been found, many in northwestern Europe. Unlike townhouses, usually lost under later buildings, the foundations of many *villas* have survived. The foundations allow us to piece together what an expensive *villa* would have looked like. In this reconstruction, the living areas are at the rear, with a colonnaded garden, while areas used for farmwork are at the front. The owner of such a *villa* might take a close interest in the farm, yet he would leave its day-to-day running to a trusted slave or *vilicus* (steward).

farming

SACRIFICE ▶
Farmers were very religious, and regularly offered prayers and sacrifices to the gods to ensure a good harvest. During the May festival of *Ambarvalia*, each farmer led a bull, a sheep, and a pig three times around his fields. The animals were then sacrificed to Mars, god of farming, who was thought to protect the fields from evil spirits. The same sacrifice, called a *suovetaurilia* – from the Latin *sus* (pig), *ovis* (sheep), and *taurus* (bull)– was also performed in Rome as a public ceremony, to protect the army and the city, as shown in this relief.

◄ LIFE ON A GREAT ESTATE

This mosaic from Carthage shows life on a farming estate owned by a rich landowner called Julius, who is the man shown seated bottom right. At the center is his large *villa*, with corner turrets, a grand gateway, and a domed bathhouse behind. At the bottom and top of the mosaic, Julius and his wife are presented with products from the estate, including wild ducks, olives, fruit, and new lambs. In the center, two men set off on a hunt with dogs and spears. The small domed building in the top right corner is a shepherd's hut. This mosaic came from Julius's *domus* in Roman Carthage. It was a reminder of his comfortable life in the country, and also served to impress visitors with his wealth.

VINES

GRAPE VARIETIES
The Romans, who loved wine, grew grapes wherever they could. They even planted vineyards in southern Britain. This 2nd-century grape mosaic comes from a dining-room floor in Tunisia.

HARVEST
Vines needed a great deal of care because they had to be pruned and supported by poles to keep the fruit off the ground. Unlike olives, which were harvested by beating the trees, every grape was hand-picked.

TREADING THE GRAPES
These two men are treading the grapes to extract the juice to make the wine. They use ropes to pull themselves up and down. The word "September" (top right) tells us when this work took place.

HARVESTING MACHINE

With a plentiful supply of slaves, the Romans had little reason to invent labor-saving devices. One of their few agricultural inventions was a harvesting machine, used in Gaul in the 1st century C.E. As this reconstruction shows, the harvester was a large toothed frame on wheels. This was pushed through a ripe cornfield by a donkey or an ox, steered by a man holding the handle at the rear. The jagged teeth cut the corn, whose ears were collected in the box.

Handle for steering

Donkey or ox stood here, its collar tied to the wooden frame

Teeth for cutting

▲ FARMING MANUALS

Several Roman farming manuals have survived, giving detailed practical instructions on running a farm. They also offer religious advice, saying which gods to pray to at different times of the year. The manuals were written not just for instruction, but also to be read aloud for entertainment. Farming was also a popular subject for poetry and art, appearing in many mosaics, such as this scene of harvested grapes being transported by oxcart.

◄ NEW FOODS

One advantage of being conquered by the Romans was a more varied diet. Under their rule, the British, for example, were introduced to a variety of fruit and vegetables, including the cabbage, onion, leek, carrot, cucumber, parsnip, turnip, radish, celery, plum, and cherry. This fresco from the 1st century AD shows figs, whose seeds have been found at Roman sites in Britain.

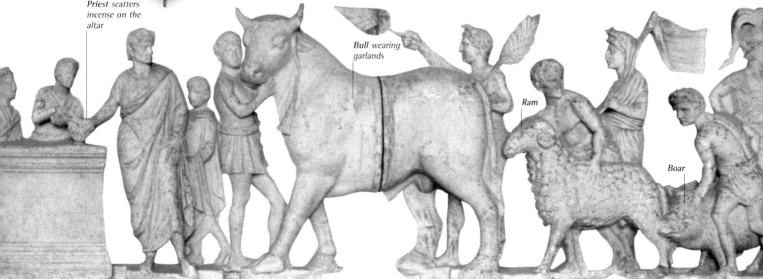

Priest scatters incense on the altar

Bull wearing garlands

Ram

Boar

ROMAN GODS

The Romans believed in many different gods, who watched over every part of life. They ranged from small household gods, who guarded doorways, to state gods, many of which matched the Greek gods. Jupiter, the sky god and special protector of the Roman state, was the same as the Greek god Zeus. His wife and sister Juno, goddess of women and childbirth, was the equivalent of the Greek goddess Hera. Ceremonies were overseen by priests, who were organized into colleges, or brotherhoods. The chief priest, called the *Pontifex Maximus*, was the emperor himself.

Oak-leaf crown

Staff topped with an eagle

Thunderbolt held in left hand

JUPITER'S TEMPLE

Jupiter's terra-cotta statue sits on a throne behind this door

Sacrificer holds axe to kill the bull

Priest wears spiked hat

Piper

Marcus Aurelius

Youth holds box with incense

Small altar

SACRIFICE ▲

Gods were worshipped in the open air, outside temples that housed their statues. Offerings of incense and animal sacrifices were made at an altar in front of the temple. This relief shows Emperor Marcus Aurelius overseeing a sacrifice in front of Jupiter's temple. While a pipe plays, the emperor scatters incense on the altar and prays to the god, asking him to keep Rome safe. His head is covered with his toga as a sign of respect for the god. A white bull waits patiently in the background before it is sacrificed.

▲ JUPITER

The temple to Jupiter Optimus Maximus ("Best and Greatest") was on Rome's Capitoline Hill. The temple also housed statues of Juno and Minerva, the goddess of crafts, wisdom, and war. Jupiter's worship was overseen by a priest called the *Flamen Dialis*, who wore a strange hat with an olive spike on top. He was forbidden to go anywhere in public without this hat. A priest called Sulpicius was deprived of his priesthood when his hat fell off while he was making a sacrifice.

gods

VESTA ►

The goddess of the hearth, Vesta, was the only Roman deity to be served by priestesses rather than priests. The six priestesses, known as the Vestal Virgins, were chosen as children from Rome's leading families. It was an honor to be selected but they had to do the job for 30 years and were not allowed to marry. They lived together in a house by Vesta's temple, where their chief duty was to tend the temple's sacred fire. The goddess's Greek name was Hestia.

A WORLD FULL OF GODS ►

Romans had dozens of gods, each of whom had a purpose. Doorways alone were protected by three different gods: Forculus (doors), Cardea (hinges), and Limentinus (the threshold). This wall painting shows Flora, one of 11 different gods who watched over cereal plants. The gods were called Proserpina (seeds), Seia (planted seeds), Nodutus (shoots), Volutina (tops), Patelana (opened sheaths), Hostilina (ears), Flora (flowers), Lacturnus (swelling heads), Matuta (ripe grain), Runcina (harvested grain), and Tutilina (stored grain).

◄ HELP FROM THE GODS

People who made offerings to gods expected practical favors in return. Almost 200 lead tablets have been found in a temple to Mercury in Uley, Gloucestershire, England. In one of the tablets, a man called Honoratus complains that four of his cows have been stolen. He asks the god not to allow the thief "to lie down or sit or drink or eat" until he has returned the cows.

CURSE TABLET

OTHER GODS

DIANA
Diana was an ancient Roman moon goddess who came to be identified with Artemis, the Greek goddess of hunting and wild animals. She was especially worshipped by women and slaves, and was thought to help mothers give birth safely. As in this wall painting, she is usually shown carrying a bow and arrow.

NEPTUNE
Like his Greek counterpart Poseidon, Jupiter's brother Neptune was the god of the sea. Riding in a chariot pulled by seahorses, Neptune was a favorite subject for mosaics, especially in places such as bathhouses. The midsummer festival of *Neptunalia* was held in his honor to prevent springs and waters from drying up.

MERCURY
Taking his name from the word *mercari* ("to trade"), Mercury was the god of merchants and travelers. He took on all the features of the Greek god Hermes, including a winged hat and sandals. Romans kept small statuettes like this one in a household shrine, hoping that Mercury would help them to make money.

MARS
Mars was originally a god of farming who later became a war god, identified with the Greek Ares. He had 24 priests called *sallii* ("leapers"). On the god's birthday in March—the month named after him—they danced through the streets of Rome carrying ancient shields, one of which was thought to have dropped from the sky.

MINERVA
Goddess of crafts and wisdom, Minerva was originally an Etruscan goddess, worshipped in Falerii. When the Romans conquered Falerii, they carried away her statue and took her back to Rome. She merged with the Greek Athena, taking on her role as a war goddess. This bronze statuette shows her wearing a Greek helmet.

| NEW MOON | FIRST QUARTER | WAXING (SLOWLY GROWING) GIBBOUS (LATIN FOR HUMPED) | FULL MOON | THIRD QUARTER |

Gnomon or pointer

THE ROMAN CALENDAR

One of the Romans' greatest achievements was
to create a calendar that is still used today. Before
they had their empire, hundreds of different dating
systems were being used around the Mediterranean.
For example, every Greek city had its own calendar,
with months named after local religious festivals. The
Romans created and named our months of the year.
They also introduced the seven-day week. Days were
named after Roman gods, which were also heavenly
bodies. Saturday, for example, is the day of Saturn.

▲ WATCHING THE MOON
The simplest way to mark time passing is by watching the phases of the moon, which go through a cycle lasting around 29 days (see above). In earliest Roman times, the start of each month was marked by the appearance of a new moon. When the priest saw the new moon, he announced that a new month had started. Romans called the first day of each month the *Kalends* from the Latin word *calare*, "to call together." The word "calendar" came from this custom. In the 5th century B.C.E., the Romans separated their months from the lunar cycle, giving them a set number of days.

SUNDIAL BESIDE THE TEMPLE OF APOLLO, POMPEII

Each day was marked with a letter A to H

EID stands for Ides, the 13th or 15th day of the month

NON stands for Nones, the ninth day before the Ides

Each double column of letters represents a Roman month

◄ TELLING THE TIME
The Romans divided day and night into 24 hours. However, since they measured the day from sunrise to sunset, the length of hours varied from season to season. In winter, the sun shines for a much shorter time each day than in summer. So winter daylight hours were shorter than those of summer. Time was measured using sundials, such as this one on an Ionic column. As the sun crosses the sky, the shadow from the gnomon (pointer) moves across the sundial. At midday, when the sun reaches its highest position, the shadow points directly downward. There were also water clocks, which used the flow of water to set off bells, move mechanical birds, and blow whistles, on the hour.

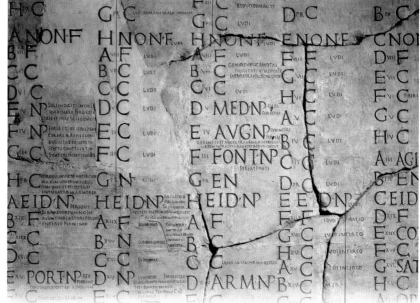

Inscription with the names of the men who set up the sundial

e▶▶ calendar

▲ ROMAN DAYS
The Romans had religious reasons for developing their calendar. They believed that certain days were marked out by the gods for particular activities. It was extremely unlucky to hold public assemblies or law cases, for example, on a day devoted to religious worship. This is a Roman calendar, inscribed on stone, using letters to indicate different types of day. The letter "C" stands for *dies comitialis* (public assembly day), when assemblies could be held. "F" stands for *dies fastus* (lawful day), when law cases could be held, while "N" denotes *dies nefastus* (unlawful day), when neither law courts nor assemblies could be held. The word "day" comes from the Latin *dies*.

NP denotes a great public festival

WANING (SLOWLY SHRINKING) GIBBOUS

WANING CRESCENT

Floor mosaic from the 2nd century C.E.

MONTHLY EVENTS

MARCH
There were only ten months in the early calendar. The Roman year originally began in March, named after Mars, the god of war and farming. This is why months named after Latin numbers—September (seventh), October (eighth), November (ninth), and December (tenth)—are counted from March, rather than January.

JANUARY
An early king, Numa Pompilius, was thought to have added two new months to the calendar, January and February. January was named after Janus, a god with two faces. He was the god of entrances and beginnings. With one face he looked back to the old year, while with the other he looked forward to the new one.

APRIL
The Romans themselves were unsure of the origin of April. According to the poet Ovid, the month was sacred to Venus, goddess of love (left). The month's name may come from her Greek name, Aphrodite. Another idea was that the name comes from *aperire* ("to open"), suggesting the opening of spring buds.

MAY AND JUNE
There were also Roman arguments about the origins of May and June. These may have been named in honor of young men (*juniors*) and older men (*maiors*), or after two goddesses, Maia and Juno. Whatever its origin, June was dedicated to Juno, goddess of marriage, shown here with her sacred bird, a peacock.

AUGUST
Emperor Augustus renamed *Sextilis* ("sixth month") August after himself, for he believed that this was his lucky month. It was in August 30 B.C.E. that his enemies, Mark Antony and Cleopatra, both killed themselves. The following August he returned in triumph to Rome. He could not foresee that he would also die in August.

▲ TRACKING THE SEASONS
This mosaic shows the different seasons, caused by the Earth's journey around the Sun. This takes 365.25 days, and is called a solar year. Until the 1st century B.C.E., the Roman calendar year had just 355 days. To keep track of the seasons, an extra month was supposed to be added every two years by the chief priest. Yet this was done so clumsily that, by the time of Julius Caesar, the calendar year was three months ahead of the solar year. To solve this problem, Caesar declared that 46 BC would have 445 days, in order to bring the calendars back in line. Thereafter, he added extra days to all the shorter months to bring the total up from 355 to 365. Because the solar year includes one-quarter of a day, he also introduced the leap year—adding an extra day to February every four years.

▲ FESTIVALS
The Roman year included dozens of major religious festivals. On February 15, for example, there was the *Lupercalia*, a festival in honor of the she-wolf that nursed Romulus and Remus. It was named after the Lupercal (wolf cave), where she suckled the twins. The festival began with the sacrifice of a dog and two goats. Two noble youths then made themselves loincloths and whips from the skins of the goats, and ran through the streets of Rome striking everyone they met. This modern painting shows women offering themselves to be struck, for they believed that this would help them become pregnant. February gets its name from the *februum*, or whip, each man carried.

EMPEROR WORSHIP

Like gods, emperors were offered worship, with their own temples, priests, and ceremonies. People sacrificed to the *genius*, or life force, of the living emperor, while many emperors, including Augustus, Claudius, Vespasian, Titus, Hadrian, and Antoninus Pius were worshipped as gods after their death. Yet few people believed that an emperor was a god in the same way as Jupiter. Emperor worship was a way of showing loyalty to the Roman state. For a new emperor, declaring that his predecessor was a god increased his own prestige. He could now call himself "son of a god", and look forward to being worshipped as a god when he died.

▲ AUGUSTUS
The first Roman emperor, Augustus, was also the first one to be worshipped as a god after his death. In this cameo we see him wearing an oak-leaf wreath and carrying a staff with an eagle on top. The eagle and oak were both sacred to Jupiter, king of the gods, so this is meant to show Augustus's godlike power.

Consecratio *(the act of making sacred)*

Funeral pyre

◄ FUNERAL PYRE
This coin, issued by Marcus Aurelius, shows the funeral pyre of Antoninus Pius, whom he had deified (declared a god). The reverse of the coin shows the four tiers of the pyre, like a wedding cake, decorated with garlands. An eagle, Jupiter's bird, was released when the pyre was set on fire. It was thought to represent the soul of the emperor joining his fellow gods.

Figure holding the Egyptian obelisk represents the Campus Martius

Antoninus Pius holds a staff topped with Jupiter's eagle

Pair of eagles carry the couple's souls

Winged god carries the couple to heaven

Roma, the goddess of the city, waves goodbye to them

Romulus and Remus, founders of Rome, decorate her shield

▲ APOTHEOSIS
This carved relief shows the journey to heaven of Emperor Antoninus Pius and his wife Faustina, who was also deified after death. This formed the base of a column, now lost, celebrating the emperor's life. The couple fly up from the Campus Martius, the open space in Rome where imperial funerals were held. You can also see the two eagles released to carry their souls. This was called an apotheosis (transformation into a god).

VESPASIAN

HADRIAN'S WIFE

In 137 C.E., Emperor Hadrian's wife of 37 years, Sabina, died. He had her deified, despite the fact that they hated each other. Hadrian was even rumored to have poisoned her. He had only married Sabina because she was the niece of Trajan, the previous emperor. He complained that if he were a private citizen and not emperor, he would have divorced her for her disagreeable character. She in turn is said to have been pleased that they never had a child, since any offspring of Hadrian would be a monster. This relief shows her being carried up to heaven by a winged goddess. She is watched by Hadrian, no doubt pleased to see her go.

▲ EMPERORS' ATTITUDES

Emperors had different attitudes to being worshipped. The insane Caligula seemed to have believed he really was a god. He enjoyed dressing up as Jupiter, wearing a golden beard and carrying a gold thunderbolt. The down-to-earth Vespasian, however, did not take it seriously. On his deathbed he joked, "Oh dear, I seem to be turning into a god!"

emperors

ANTINOUS ►

Hadrian also deified one of his close friends, Antinous, a Greek who drowned in the Nile River in 130 C.E. aged just 18. Desperate with grief at his death, Hadrian founded a new city in his honour, Antinoopolis, near the spot where he drowned. Antinous was a popular god and people felt close to him, even wearing his likeness as a lucky charm. At least 28 cities had temples to Antinous, and statues of him were mass-produced in Antinoopolis. This porphyry statue, showing him dressed as an Egyptian god, is one of 70 to survive.

Inscription records that the temple was completed in 138 C.E., the year of Hadrian's death

Hadrian's statue stood behind these Corinthian columns

Marble

◄ IN THE EAST

Emperor worship was particularly popular in the Greek-speaking east, where there was a long tradition of offering divine honors to living kings. Greek cities competed to build beautiful temples to living emperors to win their favor. This temple in Ephesus (in what is now Turkey) is one of many built for the worship of Hadrian, who loved Greece. The Greeks also built the temple in Cyzicus in Asia Minor for Hadrian—the biggest temple in the whole empire, with columns 70 ft (21 m) high.

Empty bases are for statues of a later emperor, Diocletian, and his three corulers

IN THE EAST

Two eastern provinces, Egypt and Judaea, stood
out from the rest of the Roman empire because
of religious ideas. Egypt, the world's oldest
civilization, had the most complex religion, with
hundreds of gods, portrayed in art with animal
heads. The Egyptians were happy to worship
the emperor, because they had a 3,000-year-old
belief that their pharaoh, or king, was divine.
In Judaea, the land of the Jews, however, it
was a different matter. The Jews believed that
there was only one God and they were horrified
at the idea of worshipping a human being.
Everyday life among the Jews was governed by
religious rules, which Romans found baffling.
These included prohibitions against eating pork
and making religious images.

PYRAMIDS
The Romans were fascinated by Egypt,
and many tourists traveled to see the
pharaohs' pyramid tombs. Around
12 B.C.E., a wealthy Roman called Caius
Cestius built himself a pyramid-shaped
tomb in Rome, which was 89 ft (27 m)
high. Unlike Egyptian pyramids, which
were made of stone, this one is made
of concrete faced with brick.

◄ MUMMY PORTRAIT
The Egyptians had an ancient custom of
preserving their dead as mummies, so that they
could live again in the afterlife. The Romans
continued this practice. The process
of mummification involved drying
the corpse using a type of salt,
coating it in resin, and wrapping
it in bandages. The Romans
introduced the custom of adding
realistic portraits to the mummy
casing, such as this one of a
young man called Artemidorus.
These are perhaps the finest
paintings to survive from the
ancient world.

Egyptian gods

Hawk's head

*General's cloak
(paludamentum)*

ROMAN HORUS ►
Egypt was one of the richest
provinces in the Roman empire
and was ruled by the emperor as
his personal estate. As pharaoh, he
was offered divine honors by the
Egyptian priests, who believed him
to be the human form of their
hawk-headed sky god, Horus.
Although Romans found the
idea of gods with the heads
of animals strange, their
influence can be seen
in this pottery figure of
Horus. He is dressed as
a Roman general, with
feathers suggesting armor.

OBELISK
Romans also admired Egyptian obelisks,
which represented the rays of the sun
god to Egyptians. Some 13 Egyptian
obelisks were brought back to Rome,
where they decorated racetracks and
other public spaces. This one was
erected by Emperor Augustus, who
had an inscription commemorating his
conquest of Egypt written on the base.

Temple sanctuary, contains Holy of Holies

Bronze gate

Court of the Women – the furthest point women could go

▲ HEROD THE GREAT

From 37-4 B.C.E., Judaea was ruled on behalf of the Romans by a "client king," named Herod the Great, who had been placed on the throne by Mark Antony. To win favor with his Jewish subjects, Herod rebuilt the ancient temple in Jerusalem on a massive scale. This became the focus of worship, where sacrifices were offered to God by Jews from Judaea and other lands. Since religious images were forbidden to Jews, the temple's most important room—where God was thought to be powerfully present—was kept empty. It was called the Holy of Holies. All that remains of the temple today is the Western (Wailing) Wall.

CALIGULA

◄ DIRECT RULE

In 6 C.E., Judaea was brought under direct Roman rule. This marked the beginning of a period of misgovernment, with the Romans showing no sensitivity to Jewish religious beliefs. In 39 C.E., Emperor Caligula demanded to have his statue placed in the temple and worshipped. A huge crowd of Jews gathered in Jerusalem to protest to the Roman governor. They told him that if he set up such a statue he would have to sacrifice all Jews first. When the governor, Petronius, delayed putting Caligula's plan into operation, the emperor ordered him to kill himself. Luckily for Petronius and the Jews, news that Caligula had been murdered reached Judaea before this order.

eastern provinces

REBELLION ►

A great rebellion finally broke out in 66 C.E., when the Jews seized Jerusalem and large areas of Judaea and the neighboring land of Galilee. It took the Romans more than six years to crush the rebellion. Jerusalem finally fell in 70 C.E. after an eight-month siege commanded by the future emperor Titus. The temple was burned down, and its treasures brought back to Rome, where they were paraded through the city in a triumphal procession, shown here.

Menorah, a sacred candleholder with seven branches

Signs describe the treasures

RELIEF FROM THE ARCH OF TITUS

MASADA ►

The last stronghold of the Jewish rebels was the rocky citadel of Masada, where Herod had built a fortified palace. In early 73 C.E., after a six-month siege, the Romans were on the point of capturing Masada when the 960 defenders committed mass suicide. First the men killed their wives and children, and then drew lots to kill each other. Today, Masada is a national shrine, where recruits to the Israeli army swear oaths of loyalty.

Storehouses

Bathhouse

Western Palace

Northern Palace (on three levels)

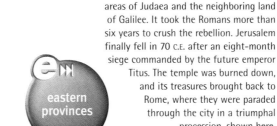

NEW GODS

The Romans always welcomed new gods. In their view the more gods the empire had to protect it, the better, and when they conquered new lands, they took over the local gods. They also turned to "mystery religions" from the east, which offered a more intense emotional experience than traditional Roman religion. Many of these foreign cults involved secret ceremonies, music, dance, and a shared holy meal. To take part, people had to undergo rites during which they were initiated (brought into) the religion. They promised never to reveal the ceremonies to outsiders.

▲ SOL INVICTUS
The worship of Sol Invictus, the unconquerable sun, was introduced from Syria in 270 C.E. by the Emperor Aurelian, who declared him to be the chief Roman god. Sol Invictus was particularly popular with emperors, who saw themselves as earthly representatives of the mighty sun. The god was always depicted wearing a radiant sun crown, as were many of the emperors on their coins. Sunday, the day of the sun, was sacred to the god.

▲ CYBELE
Also known as the Great Mother, Cybele was a goddess of nature and fertility from Phrygia, in what is now Turkey. Her worship was brought to Rome in 204 B.C.E., when a prophecy warned that the Romans would lose their war with Carthage unless they had her on their side. A sacred stone, representing the goddess, was brought to Rome from her home, Pessinus. Cybele's enthusiastic followers would dance through the streets in a frenzy, uttering wild cries and playing flutes, drums, and cymbals.

Sphinx

Sistrum

Chief priest carries a golden vessel

Conducts the singing

Priest fans the flames on the altar

Ibis, a sacred bird kept in the temple

Musician plays a pair of pipes

◄ ISIS
This painting from Herculaneum shows followers of another eastern goddess, Isis, who came from Egypt. Her priests have linen robes and shaved heads, just like Egyptian priests. The ordinary worshippers stand in two lines, singing hymns praising the goddess, while musicians play pipes and shake sacred rattles, called *sistra*. In the background is Isis's temple, guarded by a pair of Egyptian sphinxes. Isis was said to have brought her murdered brother Osiris back to life using magic. She promised the same victory over death to her worshippers, who hoped to be united with her in the next world.

gods

*Phrygian hat shows
Mithras's eastern origin*

MARBLE STATUE OF MITHRAS

Dagger

▲ MYSTERY RELIGIONS

Unlike traditional Roman religions, whose ceremonies were performed in the open air, mystery religions had secret ceremonies that took place indoors, to keep them private. People did not write about these secret ceremonies, so much of our knowledge about what went on comes from clues found in art. These wall paintings come from a house in Pompeii, called the Villa of the Mysteries. They show female worshippers of Dionysus, the Greek god of wine and ecstasy, performing an initiation ceremony.

◄ MITHRAS

After the 1st century B.C.E., one of the most popular cults centered on Mithras, the Persian god of light. More than 1,000 sculptures of him have been found, usually in the act of killing a bull. The bull's flowing blood was thought to give life to the universe. Mithras was another god who promised a glorious afterlife to his initiates.

MITHRAEUM

The sculpture of the bull being slayed occupied the most important place in every *Mithraeum*, the dark hall where the god's initiates met to perform ceremonies. Thought to represent the cave where Mithras killed the bull, the *Mithraeum* included benches where the worshippers sat to share a sacred meal. Open to men only, Mithraism was popular with soldiers and merchants, who helped spread the cult throughout the empire.

CHRISTIANITY

Like Mithraism, Christianity was another eastern religion, which spread across the Roman empire in the 1st and 2nd centuries C.E. Christians were followers of a Jewish holy man called Yeshua, better known today by the Greek form of his name, Jesus. His followers believed that he was the Messiah ("anointed one"), a long-awaited saviour sent by God. The Greek word for Messiah is *Christos*, and so he came to be called Christ. The belief developed that Jesus was the Son of God, who had risen from the dead, and who promised eternal life to his initiates. Another strongly held belief was that he would shortly return to Earth, to establish his kingdom.

Halo

Iron nail

Heelbone

HEELBONE OF JOHANAAN

◄ CRUCIFIXION
Jesus, who attracted crowds of followers, was seen as a threat to law and order by the Romans. In about 30 C.E., he was crucified by the Roman governor, Pontius Pilate. Crucifixion was an agonizing and humiliating death reserved for slaves and rebels, who were nailed to a wooden cross and left to die by suffocation. Jesus was just one of thousands of Jews to be crucified by the Romans. The skeleton of one victim, called Johanaan, was discovered in Israel in 1968, and showed how victims were nailed to a cross.

Scroll with rules of the desert community

▲ DEAD SEA SCROLLS
In 1947, a collection of Jewish scrolls dating from the time of Jesus was discovered in a cave near the Dead Sea, in Israel. Many were written by members of a Jewish religious community living in the desert. These people had much in common with the first Christians. Like them, they believed that they were living at a time when ancient Jewish prophecies would be fulfilled. They expected a Messiah who would "restore sight to the blind, raise the dead, and bring good news to the poor."

▲ PAUL
Christ's earliest followers were Jews who continued to worship in the Jerusalem temple and to obey Jewish laws. They did not see themselves as followers of a new religion. Christianity was given a new start by Paul, a Jew from Tarsus (in present-day Turkey), who was also a Roman citizen. According to Paul, Jesus offered eternal life to those who believed in him. Paul preached his message to gentiles (non-Jews) as well as Jews. He traveled widely around the eastern Mediterranean, founding new Christian communities. Paul was executed around 64 C.E., during Emperor Nero's great persecution of Christians.

Christ depicted with the head of a donkey on a cross

▲ THE FAITH SPREADS

Christianity spread rapidly, due to its powerful message that justice would be established on Earth. Unlike Mithraism, which was for men only, Christianity welcomed everyone—male and female, the free and slaves alike. Yet the idea of worshipping a crucified criminal struck many Romans as absurd. The earliest image of Christ on a cross is this mocking cartoon, scratched on a wall in Rome. It shows a donkey-headed Christ on a cross with a worshipper in front of him. The writing says, "Alexamenos worships (his) god."

▲ PERSECUTION

Christians refused to worship any Roman gods, whom they saw as demons. Their refusal to sacrifice to the emperor was seen as treason. They also aroused suspicion by meeting in secret, fueling wild rumors about what they got up to. One Roman writer, Minucius Felix, complained that Christians "spit upon the gods, they ridicule our sacred rites." From the time of Nero, Christians were regularly persecuted. This painting shows Christians thrown to wild animals in the Colosseum.

Christianity

Shining halo indicates he has become a saint

MARTYRS ►

The Romans found that killing Christians did not stop Christianity from spreading. In fact, Christians willingly accepted martyrdom, or dying for their beliefs. They thought that a public death would show people the strength of their faith, and win new converts. Many were eager to share Christ's own painful death, believing that this would help them get to heaven more quickly. Here three Christian martyrs are being executed by beheading.

CHRISTIAN SYMBOLS

FISH
Early Christian art often used coded images, such as that of the fish. The letters of the Greek word for fish, *Ichthys*, stand for "Jesus Christ, God's Son, Savior" in Greek. The anchor resembles a cross and represents a Christian's faith—something to hold onto firmly in a stormy world.

SHEPHERD
Christ was also portrayed as a shepherd, caring for his flock, or followers. Christ was said to have compared himself to a "good shepherd," who had come to save lost sheep. This shepherd is a carving on an early Christian sarcophagus (stone coffin).

CHI-RHO
Another Christian symbol was made up of the first two letters of the word "Christ" in Greek—X (*Chi*) and P (*Rho*). The two letters were combined to make the "Chi-Rho" symbol shown in gold on this piece of silverware, which was owned by a Christian living in Roman Britain.

ENEMIES OF ROME

In the 3rd century C.E., the Roman empire came under attack from all sides. Germanic tribes broke through the northern frontiers, raiding as far west as Spain. At the same time a new, strong Persian Empire threatened from the east. A series of Roman emperors was unable to provide strong leadership. Between 235 and 284 C.E., there were 21 official rulers, and many more pretenders—men who tried but failed to seize power. Almost all of them died violent deaths, often at the hands of their own soldiers.

▲ NEW CITY WALLS

By the middle of the 3rd century, the Roman Empire was threatened by large confederations (groupings) of Germanic peoples, called the Franks, Alemanni, Vandals, and Goths. These tribes swept over the Rhine making deep raids into the empire. In response, many Roman cities built massive walls to try to keep them out. This is a section of the Aurelian Wall in Rome, begun by Emperor Aurelian in 271 C.E.

THE SASSANIAN EMPIRE ▶

Rome was now threatened by an equally powerful empire, in the east. This was the new Persian Empire created by the Sassanian family of kings. King Shapur I, who ruled from 241–72 C.E., was the deadliest enemy Rome had faced since the Carthaginian general Hannibal. Leading vast armies, whose strength lay in heavily armored cavalrymen, Shapur made yearly raids on Roman territory, as well as leading three great campaigns against the empire. In his coin portrait, he wears a crown with a distinctive globe, called a *korymbos*.

QUEEN ZENOBIA

The most famous enemy of Rome was Queen Zenobia of Palmyra, a Syrian desert kingdom, which she ruled on behalf of her young son, Septimius Vaballathus. Zenobia saw Rome's difficulties as a wonderful opportunity to expand her kingdom. In 269 C.E., she conquered Egypt and the following year took over most of Asia Minor. In 272 C.E., the Roman emperor, Aurelian, led an army against her and took her as his prisoner. She was taken to Rome and made to take part in Aurelian's triumphal procession, where she was paraded in golden chains. Yet the emperor, a merciful man, decided to spare her life. She was given an elegant villa in Tibur (Tivoli) outside Rome, where she spent her last years. This 18th-century painting by the Italian artist Giovanni Tiepolo shows Zenobia being presented to Aurelian as his captive.

Valerian in Roman dress kneels before Shapur

Shapur on horseback wearing a tall crown

▲ AN EMPEROR'S HUMILIATION

Shapur's greatest triumph came in 260 C.E., when he captured Emperor Valerian in battle. Shapur was so delighted he had huge rock carvings made, depicting the emperor's surrender. He added an inscription boasting that he had taken Valerian prisoner with his own hands. According to the Roman writer, Lactantius, Shapur used Valerian as a human mounting block, stepping on his neck whenever he mounted his horse. After Valerian's death, Shapur had him skinned, dyed purple, and stuffed, to be put on permanent display in a temple. The capture of an emperor was a terrible blow to Rome's prestige.

enemies

BREAKAWAY EMPIRE ▶
Following the capture of Valerian, his son and coruler, Gallienus, faced widespread rebellions. In 260 C.E., a Roman commander on the Rhine named Postumus founded a breakaway empire centered on Gaul, Britain, and Spain. Postumus had his own capital Trier, in Germany, had coins minted bearing his portrait, and successfully defended his empire against both Germanic invaders and Gallienus. Despite these successes, Postumus was murdered by his own soldiers in 269 C.E.

Pure gold coin showing Emperor Aurelian.

◀ AURELIAN
Effective Roman rule was finally provided by Aurelian, who was proclaimed emperor by his troops in 270 C.E. After disposing of rival claimants, he defeated two invasions, by the Vandals and Alemanni. He went on to conquer Queen Zenobia's empire in 272 C.E., and the breakaway western empire in 274 C.E. After celebrating his triumph in Rome, he set off to invade Persia, only to be murdered by his soldiers in 275 C.E.

◀ DIOCLETIAN
In 284 C.E., yet another general, Diocletian, was declared emperor by his troops. Realizing that the empire faced too many problems for one man, he divided it into an eastern and a western half with a senior emperor, or Augustus, and a junior emperor, or Caesar, in each. Diocletian himself was Augustus of the east. This carving of the four rulers, called "Tetrarchs," shows them clasping each other tightly, while gripping the eagle-headed hilts (handles) of their swords. The statue, which now stands outside St. Mark's Basilica in Venice, Italy, was designed as a powerful image of unity and strength.

Statue is 51 in (129.5 cm) high

DIOCLETIAN'S PALACE IN SPLIT

NEW STYLE OF RULE ▲
Diocletian introduced a new style of rule, modeled on Persian kings. He wore a pearl-studded diadem, or crown, and was addressed as *dominus* ("lord"). Visitors were expected to show their respect by kneeling before him and kissing the hem of his purple robe. This new remote style restored the emperor's prestige and also distanced him from potential murderers. Diocletian finally abdicated after ruling for an impressive 21 years. He was the only emperor ever to give up power willingly. This is an artist's impression of the vast palace he built at Salona (Split), in what is now Croatia. He spent his last years here, where he found pleasure in a new hobby—growing cabbages.

Porphyry, a purple rock from Egypt

THE FOUR TETRARCHS

CONSTANTINE ►
Before becoming a Christian, Constantine had worshipped Sol Invictus, the sun god, and he introduced several features of sun worship into Christianity. The birthday of the sun, on December 25, now became Christ's birthday. Constantine also decreed Sunday, the sacred day of the sun, to be a Christian day of rest. This modern statue is in the English city of York, where Constantine was first proclaimed ruler by his troops.

Christian emperors

Inscription reads: "By this sign conquer"

CONSTANTINE BY THI

CHRISTIAN EMPERORS

After Emperor Diocletian retired in 305 C.E., a new series of civil wars broke out. The eventual victor was Constantine, who ruled the west starting in 312 C.E., and the whole empire starting in 324 C.E. Constantine was a Christian, and did everything he could to spread the religion. He founded a new Christian capital in the east, which was named Constantinople after himself, and which he filled with churches. For the Christians, who had been persecuted for years, this was an almost unbelievable turn of events. Now it was an advantage to be a Christian, because the emperor filled the most important posts at his court with fellow believers. Under Constantine, and the Christian emperors who followed him, there were mass conversions to the faith. Even so, many people remained loyal to their old gods, and would not give them up without a long struggle.

THE CHURCH MEETS IN NICAEA ►
Constantine was horrified to discover that many Christians were bitterly divided. They had fierce arguments with each other about basic beliefs, such as how Jesus Christ could be both a human and God. In 325 C.E., Constantine summoned a great council of Church leaders to Nicaea, a city in Anatolia (now part of Turkey), to work out a common creed, or set of beliefs. Those who refused to accept it were persecuted. This 18th-century Russian painting shows the Church leaders at Nicaea, watched by Constantine and his mother.

Sword is held to resemble a cross

CHRIST MOSAIC ▶

The influence of Constantine and Sol Invictus on the image of Christ can be seen in this mosaic from Hinton St. Mary, in Dorset. The mosaic from the 4th century C.E. shows a clean-shaven Christ. He shares the same hairstyle as Constantine and Sol Invictus. He also has lines shooting out from behind his head, like the radiant crown of the sun god. However, these lines are formed by the first two letters of Christ's name in Greek: *Chi* (X) and *Rho* (P). The two pomegranates symbolize Christ's victory over death.

NEW CHURCHES ▶

The new state religion required new buildings for communal worship. These had to be big, to hold the growing numbers of converts to Christianity. Unlike a temple, where worship took place in the open air, Christians worshipped inside the building, so this was where the richest decoration lay, with mosaics and wall paintings. This church in Rome, lined with Corinthian columns, is dedicated to St. Sabina, a Christian martyr. Built in around 430 C.E., it is modeled on a basilica, a Roman hall used as a law court.

JULIAN THE APOSTATE ▶

Constantine's nephew Julian had been brought up a Christian, but secretly came to prefer the old gods. When he became emperor in 361 C.E., he tried hard to bring back the old faith—restoring temples, appointing priests, and sacrificing thousands of animals to the gods. He also wrote books criticizing Christian beliefs, which struck him as foolish. Yet he refused to persecute Christians, believing that they should be pitied rather than hated. The Christians called him "the apostate," which means someone who has abandoned their faith. Julian was killed fighting the Persians in 363 C.E.

TEMPLES DESTROYED ▶

The Christian emperors who ruled after Julian made it increasingly difficult to worship the old Roman gods. In 391 C.E., Emperor Theodosius passed a law closing all the temples. Throughout the empire, Christians seized the chance to attack temples and smash statues of gods. In 401 C.E., John Chrysostom, Bishop of Constantinople, led an attack on the Temple of Diana (Artemis) in Ephesus in what is now Turkey. The temple, regarded as one of the Seven Wonders of the World, was torn to the ground. Yet Christians still feared the power of Diana—now thought of as a demon—and carved crosses on the walls of Ephesus to protect themselves from her.

Last remaining column of ruined Temple in Ephesus

HUNS ATTACK ALANS, A GERMANIC PEOPLE

THE FALL OF THE WEST

In the late 4th century C.E., a fierce nomadic people called the Huns left their homeland on the plains of Central Asia and swept west, attacking the Germanic peoples living north of the Danube. This Hun onslaught set off a mass movement of Germanic peoples, who overwhelmed the defenses of the Roman empire. The incomers included Visigoths, Ostrogoths, Vandals, Franks, Burgundians, Angles, Saxons, and Jutes, who all conquered and settled Roman territory. As a result, in the 5th century C.E., the western Roman Empire collapsed.

FLATTENED SKULL
OF A HUN

HUNS ▲

Unlike the Germanic peoples, who had adopted many features of Roman society, the Huns were different in every possible way. They were nomads—people who were constantly on the move, spending most of their lives on horseback. With their Asiatic features and animal-skin clothes they even looked different from Romans. They also flattened their heads, which they did by tightly binding babies' skulls while they were still soft. To the Romans, the Huns were savages. One writer, Ammianus Marcellinus, wrote, "They are so ugly and bent that they might be two-legged animals."

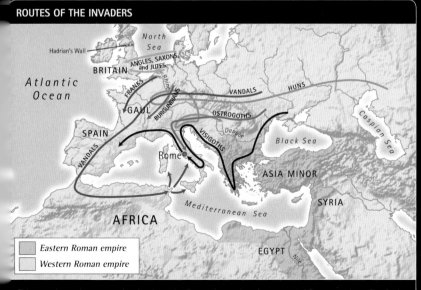

ROUTES OF THE INVADERS

North Sea
Hadrian's Wall
BRITAIN — ANGLES, SAXONS, and JUTES
Atlantic Ocean
FRANKS
GAUL
BURGUNDIANS
VANDALS
HUNS
OSTROGOTHS
SPAIN
VISIGOTHS
Danube
VANDALS
Rome
Black Sea
Caspian Sea
ASIA MINOR
Mediterranean Sea
SYRIA
AFRICA
EGYPT
Nile

Eastern Roman empire
Western Roman empire

This map shows the routes taken by the major Germanic peoples who conquered Roman territory. The Goths, who had attacked the empire in the 3rd century C.E., were now divided into two peoples: the Visigoths, who invaded Italy before founding a kingdom in Spain, and the Ostrogoths, who founded their own kingdom in Italy. Meanwhile, North Africa fell to the Vandals. The map also shows the route of the Huns, who raided Gaul and Italy before conquering their own ... north of the Danube.

▲ VISIGOTHS

In AD 376, the Visigoths, terrified of the Huns, begged the eastern emperor Valens (shown on this coin) to let them shelter inside the empire. Valens agreed, yet treated the Visigoths so badly that they rebelled against him. In AD 378, Valens marched against the Visigoths, who had now been joined by the Ostrogoths. Valens and most of his army were killed at the Battle of Adrianople (now ...

STILICHO ▶
In the 4th century C.E., the defense of the Roman empire increasingly depended on Romanized Germanic soldiers. In 395 C.E., Stilicho, a Vandal by birth, became guardian of the young western emperor, Honorius. In 402 C.E., Stilicho defeated the invading Visigoths and drove them out of Italy. Stilicho was the real ruler of the west until his death in 408 C.E.

Long spear and *oval shield,* with a *central boss,* both *Germanic in origin*

Panel carved from *ebony,* a dark wood

◀ HONORIUS
An ivory plaque shows the western emperor Honorius, who ruled 395–423 C.E. He is holding a standard bearing the hopeful words, "In the name of Christ, you will always conquer." Far from doing any conquering, however, Honorius was unable to stop the Visigoths invading Italy twice. In 402 C.E., following the first invasion, Honorius abandoned the western capital, Milan, and fled to the safety of Ravenna, in northeastern Italy, which was protected by marshes.

Globe topped with a *victory goddess*

Ribbon was a Roman *general's insignia*

fall of the west

Long hair shows *Germanic origins*

Spear

▲ VANDAL LORD
The word "vandalism" now means mindless destruction. Yet the Vandals, like many other Germanic peoples, hoped to share in the wealth of the empire rather than destroy it. Even before they entered the empire, in 406 C.E., they had been partly Romanized and had adopted Christianity. In North Africa, Vandal lords lived like wealthy Romans, in villas decorated with mosaics. This mosaic shows a Vandal lord setting off on a hunt.

▲ THE SACK OF ROME
In 410 C.E., the Visigoths, led by their king, Alaric, invaded Italy for a second time. Alaric camped outside Rome, demanding vast sums of money to leave the city unharmed. One payment was made, but Alaric then lost his patience and marched on the city, which he captured on August 24. For the next three days, the Visigoths sacked Rome, stripping the city of its treasures. Yet they left most of the churches alone, because they were Christians. Although it was no longer the capital, news of the sack shocked people throughout the empire. In Palestine, St. Jerome declared in a letter, "As I dictate, sobs choke my words. The city which had taken the whole world was itself taken."

THE BYZANTINE EMPIRE

Although the western empire fell in the 5th century C.E., the eastern empire survived another 1,000 years. This became known as the Byzantine Empire, after Byzantium, the original Greek name of the city refounded as Constantinople. Although the Byzantines spoke Greek, they called themselves Romans, and thought of themselves as the heirs to Emperor Augustus. One Byzantine emperor, Justinian (ruled 527–565 C.E.), even set out to win back the lost western territories, and reconquered Italy, North Africa, and southern Spain.

▲ JUSTINIAN THE GREAT
This mosaic portrait of Justinian comes from the church of St. Apollinare in Ravenna in northern Italy, which the emperor's armies reconquered in 540 C.E. Ravenna was the capital of the Byzantine province until 751 C.E., when another Germanic people, the Lombards, captured the city, finally ending Byzantine rule in Italy.

◄ BELISARIUS
In another mosaic, a haloed Justinian walks in procession with his soldiers and courtiers. The man on Justinian's right may be the emperor's brilliant general, Belisarius, whose campaigns doubled the size of the Byzantine empire. In 533 C.E., Belisarius led an army of just 15,000 men to North Africa, where he conquered the Vandal kingdom and captured the king, Gelimer. The following year, Justinian allowed him to hold a triumphal procession, the first held in Constantinople. Belisarius went on to conquer Sicily, in 535 C.E., and Italy between 536 and 540 C.E., when he captured a second king, Vitiges of the Ostrogoths.

MOSAIC IN THE BASILICA SAN VITALE, RAVENNA

Halo

Cross

▲ UP A PILLAR
Byzantines were intensely religious, and many went to great lengths to be closer to God. This wall painting shows Saint Simeon Stylites (387–459 C.E.), who spent 36 years living on top of a tall pillar in the Syrian desert. Although he hoped to withdraw from the world, he attracted large crowds, curious to see him.

HAGIA SOPHIA ▶
Justinian was a great builder. He constructed the famous Church of Hagia Sophia ("Holy Wisdom") in Constantinople between 531 and 537 C.E. For centuries, it remained the biggest church in the world, and the size of its massive dome, 108 ft (33 m) in diameter, would not be matched until the 1430s. The interior was covered with mosaics and colored marble, lit up by light streaming through the windows. Justinian's official historian, Procopius, wrote on its completion, "The church has become a sight of marvelous beauty, overwhelming those who see it."

JUSTINIAN'S LAW CODE

By the time of Justinian (left), the Romans had been making laws for almost 1,000 years. Lawyers were expected to study not only the laws but also a mass of commentaries written by legal experts, explaining how the laws should be applied. Since these commentaries often contradicted each other, lawyers had to read as many as possible, before following the majority view. Justinian appointed a committee of lawyers to produce a new, simpler code, removing out-of-date laws and sorting out the contradictions of the commentators. His team took three years, reading more than 2,000 books containing 3,000,000 lines. One of the most influential works in history, Justinian's Law Code formed the basis of many later legal systems.

ARAB FORCES BESIEGE
A TOWN IN SICILY

▲ THE RISE OF ISLAM

In the 7th century, the Byzantines were challenged by the rise of a new religion, Islam, founded in Arabia by the prophet Muhammad (c.570–632 C.E.). Within a century of Muhammad's death, his Muslim followers had conquered North Africa and most of the Near East. With the loss of much of its richest territory, the Byzantine empire shrank to become just one of several rival states in the eastern Mediterranean.

▲ FALL OF CONSTANTINOPLE

The Byzantine empire survived in a weakened state until the 15th century, when a new Muslim people, the Ottoman Turks, invaded Europe. In 1453, the Ottomans used massive cannon to break through the great walls of Constantinople. Following its capture, the Byzantine capital was given a Turkish name, Istanbul. Many of the churches, including Hagia Sophia, were converted into Muslim prayer halls called mosques. This painting shows the Ottoman ruler, Mehmed, preparing his attack on the city.

Dome is a replacement added in the 16th century

Towers called minarets added when the church became a mosque

THE LEGACY OF ROME

The legacy of ancient Rome is so widespread that in many ways we still think and act like Romans. We use the Roman alphabet, calendar, and hundreds of words derived from Latin. The word "legacy," for example, comes from the Latin *legare*, to bequeath. Five other languages—Italian, French, Spanish, Portuguese, and Romanian—are all based on Latin. We still live in cities founded by the Romans, including Cologne, Lyons, Paris, and London. We still travel along the routes of Roman roads. Roman law underlies many western legal systems. Around the world, 2.1 billion people are believers in a late Roman religion—Christianity.

TEMPLE OF CASTOR AND POLLUX

Corinthian column 41 ft (12.5 m) tall

UNITED STATES REPUBLIC ▲
The U.S. political system, set up in the 18th century, was modeled on the Roman Republic—including a government assembly known as the Senate. The U.S. dollar bill carries Jupiter's sacred eagle, which holds a scroll in its beak bearing the Latin motto, "*E Pluribus Unum*," meaning "one (people) out of many."

◄ COINS
British coins are modeled on Roman coins, with a portrait of the monarch shown in profile, like a Roman emperor. The British have also copied the Roman custom of using abbreviated Latin words to indicate the ruler's titles. The Latin on this English pound coin spells "D.G.REG.F.D.", which is short for "*Deo Gratia Regina Fidei Defensor*"—"by the grace of God, Queen, defender of the faith."

legacy

Welsh limestone facing called Anglesey marble

◄ TEMPLES OLD AND NEW
Many public buildings, such as banks, libraries, museums, and town halls, are built in the style of Roman temples. This is Birmingham town hall, in England, built in 1834 for public meetings and musical performances. The architect, Joseph Aloysius Hansom, modeled his building on the ruined temple of Castor and Pollux, which has long been admired as one of the most beautiful structures in Rome.

Eight columns at the front, like its Roman model

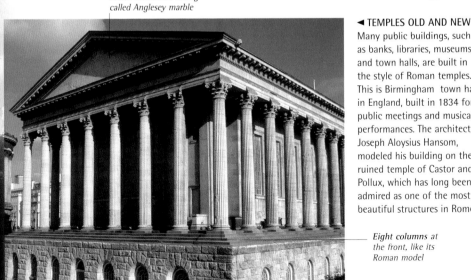

BIRMINGHAM TOWN HALL, IN ENGLAND

▲ ALPHABET

The Roman alphabet is the most widely used writing system in the world today. It is used in most of Europe, in the Americas, in Africa south of the Sahara desert, in Australia, and across the islands of the Pacific Ocean. Its use is still spreading. When the Soviet Union broke up in 1991, several of the newly formed states gave up the old Russian Cyrillic alphabet and adopted the Roman one. The alphabet has changed over time, and today the Romans would recognize only the capital letters. The lower-case letters and the letters J, U, and W, were created in the Middle Ages. The Romans would have written "Julius" as "IVLIVS".

ROMAN CATHOLIC CHURCH ►

The Roman Catholic Church, with its headquarters in Rome, preserves many Roman customs, including the burning of incense and the wearing of robes based on late Roman ones. This is the head of the Roman Catholic Church, Pope Benedict XVI, who is still known as the *Pontifex Maximus*—the ancient title of Rome's chief priest. Benedict, who became Pope in 2005, hopes to revive the use of Latin in churches, saying, "Latin makes it easier for Christians from different countries to pray together."

POPE BENEDICT XVI

BULLFIGHT IN PAMPLONA, NORTHERN SPAIN

◄ BULLFIGHTING

The bullfights held in Spain and southern France are a legacy of the Roman amphitheater. Many bullfights take place in Roman amphitheaters or buildings modeled on them, such as this Spanish bullring. The ancient Romans also fought bulls, particularly during the late period, when wild animals, such as lions, became increasingly scarce. In Roman bullfights, like modern ones, bulls were goaded to make them angry by mounted fighters, called *succursores*. Those who killed the bull were called *taurarii* (from *taurus*, the Latin for bull). They fought on foot and used spears rather than the swords and red capes of modern bullfighters.

◄ IMPERIAL ARCHITECTURE

By the 19th century, many European countries had created empires of their own. They celebrated their conquests by building monuments copied from ancient Rome, including statues of generals on horseback and triumphal arches. London's Marble Arch (below), designed by John Nash and built in 1828 from the same Italian marble used in Roman arches, was modeled on Constantine's triumphal arch in Rome, built in 315 C.E.

ARCH OF CONSTANTINE, ROME

One of four statues of Dacian prisoners taken from Trajan's Arch

MARBLE ARCH, LONDON

TIMELINE

The letters C.E. stand for Common Era (or Current or Christian Era). This is a common system of numbering years starting from the year of the birth of Christ. The letters B.C.E. indicate a year Before the Common Era. The letter "c." in front of a date is an abbreviation of *circa*, meaning "about".

753 B.C.E. The date traditionally given for the original founding of the city of Rome by Romulus.

c.750 B.C.E. The first Greek migrants begin to settle in southern Italy and Sicily.

c.510 B.C.E. The Romans drive out their last king and establish a Republic.

458 B.C.E. Cincinnatus serves as dictator for 15 days and saves Rome from the invading Aequi.

390 B.C.E. Gauls capture and sack Rome.

c.378 B.C.E. The Romans build new fortification walls around their city.

343-290 B.C.E. The Romans fight and win three wars against the Samnites of central Italy.

321 B.C.E. During the Second Samnite War, a Roman army surrenders to the Samnites after being trapped in a pass called the Caudine forks.

280-275 B.C.E. Rome fights a war against King Pyrrhus of Epirus, who has invaded Italy to help the Greeks of Tarentum in the south. Pyrrhus wins two victories, but is defeated in his third battle.

264-241 B.C.E. The First Punic War, in which Rome fights Carthage for the control of Sicily. The Romans win the war, conquer Sicily, and become a great naval power.

218-201 B.C.E. The Second Punic War, in which the Carthaginian general, Hannibal, crosses the Alps to invade Italy from the north. He wins three great victories, but is unable to conquer Rome.

215-205 B.C.E. Rome is at war with King Philip V of Macedon, who has made a treaty with Hannibal.

202 B.C.E. The Roman general Scipio defeats Hannibal at the Battle of Zama, near Carthage, in North Africa.

200-197 B.C.E. The Romans fight a second war against King Philip V of Macedon. The Roman general Titus Quinctius Flamininus wins a decisive victory at Cynoscephalae in 197 B.C.E.

191-190 B.C.E. The Romans defeat King Antiochus III of Syria at Thermopylae in 191 B.C.E. and Magnesia in 190 B.C.E.

171-168 B.C.E. The third war with Macedon, which later becomes a Roman province.

149-146 B.C.E. Rome fights the Third Punic War. The war ends with the destruction of Carthage.

c.135 B.C.E. Eunus leads a slave rebellion in Sicily. This is finally crushed in 131 B.C.E.

133 B.C.E. The tribune Tiberius Gracchus attempts to distribute land to the poor. His enemies in the Senate organize a riot in which he is killed.

107 B.C.E. Gaius Marius becomes Consul for the first time, and begins reforms of the army.

104 B.C.E. Marius captures King Jugurtha of Numidia in North Africa. Marius brings the king back to Rome for his triumphal procession. Jugurtha is then executed.

102-101 B.C.E. Marius defeats two invading Germanic tribes—the Teutones and the Cimbri.

91-88 B.C.E. Rome's Italian allies rebel in what becomes knows as the Social War (from *socii*, the Latin name for allies). The Romans win over some cities by extending citizenship, and defeat the others in battle.

89 B.C.E. Marius attempts to deprive his rival, Lucius Cornelius Sulla, of an eastern command. Sulla marches on Rome and forces Marius to flee.

87-86 B.C.E. While Sulla is away in the east, Marius returns to Rome and begins to massacre his rival's supporters. He dies in 86 B.C.E., a few days after becoming consul for the seventh time.

83-79 B.C.E. The victorious Sulla returns to Rome and begins his rule as dictator.

73-71 B.C.E. The gladiator Spartacus leads a great slave rebellion against Rome.

67 B.C.E. Pompey clears the sea of pirates, capturing many of their bases in the eastern Mediterranean.

66-62 B.C.E. Pompey's eastern campaigns, in which he defeats King Mithridates of Pontus, makes Syria a Roman province, and reorganizes the government of Judaea.

58-49 B.C.E. Julius Caesar conquers Gaul.

55-54 B.C.E. Caesar leads two expeditions to Britain.

49 B.C.E. Caesar marches on Rome, starting a civil war with the leading senators, led by Pompey. The senators escape to Greece, where Pompey spends a year raising forces to fight Caesar.

48 B.C.E. Pompey is defeated by Caesar at the Battle of Pharsalus. Pompey flees to Egypt, where he is stabbed to death on the orders of the young king, Ptolemy.

45 B.C.E. Caesar finally defeats the last of the senatorial forces, in Africa and Spain, ending the civil war.

44 B.C.E. On March 15, a few weeks after being declared dictator for life, Caesar is assassinated.

42 B.C.E. Mark Antony and Octavian defeat Brutus and Cassius at Philippi. The victors divide the empire between them, with Octavian taking the west and Antony the east.

33-31 B.C.E. Civil war between Octavian and Antony ends in the latter's defeat at the Battle of Actium. Antony commits suicide and Octavian becomes sole ruler of the empire.

27 B.C.E. Octavian becomes Rome's first emperor. He is given the title Augustus ("the revered one").

14-37 C.E. After the death of Augustus, his stepson, Tiberius, rules as the second emperor.

c.30 C.E. Crucifixion of Jesus Christ, in Jerusalem.

37-41 C.E. Rule of Caligula, who is cruel and mentally unstable and demands to be worshipped as a god. He is murdered by the Praetorian Guard.

41-54 C.E. Rule of Claudius, who organizes the conquest of Britain in 43 C.E.

54-68 C.E. Rule of Nero, the last emperor from the family of Augustus. Nero murders many close family members, including his mother, stepbrother, and two wives. Following a great fire in Rome, in 64 C.E., he builds a huge new palace in the center of the city.

66 C.E. A rebellion against Roman rule breaks out in Judaea.

68 C.E. Following widespread rebellions by leading generals, Nero kills himself. A new civil war breaks out, in which Rome is ruled by four emperors in a row.

69-79 C.E. Rule of Vespasian, the first emperor of the Flavian dynasty. He organizes the construction of Rome's Colosseum.

70 C.E. Titus, son of Vespasian, captures and sacks Jerusalem following a five-month siege.

79 C.E. The volcano Vesuvius erupts, burying the towns of Herculaneum and Pompeii in western Italy.

79-81 C.E. Rule of Titus, a popular and generous emperor. The Colosseum is completed during his reign.

81-96 C.E. Rule of Titus's brother, Domitian, a cruel and hated ruler, who kills many leading Romans. He is finally murdered.

98-117 C.E. Rule of Trajan, who conquers Dacia and Iraq. By the end of his reign, the empire has reached its largest size.

117-138 C.E. Rule of Hadrian, who gives up some of Trajan's conquests and strengthens the empire's frontiers with new defenses, including Hadrian's Wall in northern Britain.

161-180 C.E. Rule of Marcus Aurelius. He spends much of his reign fighting a Germanic tribe called the Marcomanni.

180-192 C.E. Rule of Marcus Aurelius's son, Commodus, notorious for fighting as a gladiator in the Colosseum.

193-211 C.E. Rule of Septimius Severus, founder of the Severan dynasty.

211-217 C.E. Rule of Caracalla, who grants Roman citizenship to all the free inhabitants of the empire in 212 C.E.

235-284 C.E. Plague spreads through the empire, which also comes under attack from all sides. There are many emperors, who rule for short periods of time.

260 C.E. Sassanian Persian king, Shapur, captures Emperor Valerian in battle. Valerian later dies in captivity.

260-269 C.E. Postumus, a Roman general, founds a breakaway empire in the west, including Gaul, Britain, and Spain.

270-275 C.E. Rule of Aurelian, who reunites the empire, builds new walls around Rome, and sets off to fight the Persians, only to be murdered by his soldiers.

284-305 C.E. Rule of Diocletian, who divides the empire into western and eastern halves, with a senior and junior emperor in each.

312 C.E. Constantine, the first Christian emperor, defeats his rival in the west, Maxentius, at the Battle of the Milvian Bridge.

313 C.E. In Milan, Constantine issues an edict (order) ending the persecution of Christians. The eastern emperor, Licinius, accepts the edict.

324 C.E. Constantine defeats Licinius, and forces him to abdicate. The empire is now united under Constantine's rule.

330 C.E. Constantine refounds the city of Byzantium and renames it Constantinople.

361-363 C.E. Rule of Julian the Apostate, who tries but fails to restore the worship of the old gods of Rome.

376 C.E. The Visigoths enter the Roman Empire. They are given permission to stay, but are so badly treated they rise in rebellion.

378 C.E. Battle of Adrianople, in which the Visigoths defeat and kill Emperor Valens.

391 C.E. Emperor Theodosius issues a law closing all temples and banning sacrifices.

406-409 C.E. The Vandals, Alans, and Suebi cross the Rhine, sweeping across Gaul and into Spain. Roman rule in the west crumbles.

410 C.E. The Visigoths, led by King Alaric, invade Italy and sack Rome. Alaric then leads them to southern Italy, from where he plans to invade North Africa, but dies of a fever before he can do this.

429-439 C.E. The Vandals invade and conquer North Africa, capturing Carthage in 439 C.E. Their king, Geiseric the Lame, makes Carthage his royal capital.

476 C.E. Romulus Augustulus, the last emperor of the west, is overthrown by a Germanic chieftain called Odoacer, who becomes king of Italy.

527-565 C.E. Rule of the Byzantine emperor, Justinian the Great, whose armies reconquer Italy, North Africa, and southern Spain. Justinian also has a great law code drawn up, and builds the Church of Hagia Sophia in Constantinople.

1453 C.E. Constantinople, is captured by Ottoman Turks, as the last Byzantine emperor, Constantine XI, dies fighting before its walls.

GLOSSARY

Aedile Magistrate responsible for markets, streets, and public buildings. *Aediles* also put on public shows.

Amphitheater Large, oval building used for public entertainments, especially fights between gladiators. It was also used for public executions and wild-beast shows.

Amphora A two-handled pot, used for storing oil, wine, and other goods.

Aqueduct An artificial channel for carrying water to a town. Aqueducts might be underground or carried on arched bridges.

Atrium Entrance hall of a Roman house, with an opening in the roof to let in light, and an ornamental pool beneath.

Auxiliary Noncitizen soldier serving in the Roman army. Auxiliaries were paid less than citizen-soldiers. On retirement, they would be granted citizenship.

Barbarian Roman and Greek name for foreigners, who were seen as less civilized because they did not speak Latin or Greek.

Basilica A large, aisled hall, used as a law court.

Centurion Officer commanding a unit of 80 men in the Roman army. The unit is known as a century (hundred), because it was originally made up of 100 men. There were 60 centurions in each legion.

Citizen A member of a state, with greater political rights than a noncitizen. Roman citizens were offered greater legal protection than noncitizens, and male citizens had the right to vote and serve as magistrates.

Consuls The two senior Roman magistrates who, under the Republic, were the heads of state and army commanders, and who presided at meetings of the Senate.

Dictator Official given unlimited powers, usually during an emergency. Dictators normally served for only a short period and a particular purpose. One exception was Julius Caesar, who made himself dictator for life.

Domus A private house.

Dynasty A succession of rulers from one family.

Empire A large area of land, including many peoples, under a single authority.

Flamen A priest serving a god or deified emperor. The priest of Jupiter in Rome was called the *Flamen Dialis*, while the priest of Mars was the *Flamen Martialis*.

Forum The central public meeting place in any Roman town, surrounded by law courts, temples, and other public buildings.

Freedmen Freed slaves, who often continued to have ties of loyalty with their former owners. Imperial freedmen could amass great political power by controlling access to the emperor.

Gladiator Professional fighter in an amphitheater. Gladiators, who were often slaves, fought each other and against wild animals, often to the death, to entertain the public.

Hypocaust Heating system with a furnace sending hot air through spaces beneath floors and walls. Hypocausts were used to heat the hot and warm rooms of bathhouses.

Inhumation Burying the body whole, rather than cremating (burning) it. Under the empire, inhumation gradually replaced cremation as the main way of disposing of the dead.

Insula A section of housing in a Roman town.

Lararium A shrine that contained statues of the Roman household gods.

Legion Roman army of around 5,500 men. Each legion was commanded by an officer called a legate, assisted by six tribunes. Under the Roman empire, there were between 25 and 30 legions.

Ludi General name given to sports events, public games, and theatrical performances.

Mosaic Picture made from many tiny pieces of tile, stone, or glass pushed into cement.

Mystery religion A religion offering secret wisdom, which is revealed only to initiates (people who go through special rites to be brought into the faith). Mithras and Isis were both gods worshipped in mystery religions.

Paterfamilias The male head of a Roman family.

Patricians Aristocratic class of early Roman citizens.

Plebeians The common citizens of early Rome, with fewer privileges than the patricians.

Pontifex Maximus Chief priest of Roman religion, a post held by the emperor.

Praetor Highest-ranking Roman magistrate below the consuls. *Praetors* were the senior law officers.

Praetorian Guard Imperial guard based in Rome, who had their own camp to the northeast of the city.

Punic wars Wars fought between Rome and Carthage from 264 to 146 B.C.E., when the North African city was destroyed. The word "Punic" comes from the Latin name for the Phoenicians.

Quaestor Junior magistrates who controlled the treasury under the Republic. Under the empire, two *quaestors* served as assistants to the emperor, reading his speeches to the Senate.

Relief Carving in which figures stand out from a flat background.

Republic A state ruled by elected officials rather than by a king. Rome was a Republic from c.510 B.C.E. until 27 B.C.E., when Augustus became the first emperor.

Senate A body of serving and ex-magistrates, whose role was to offer advice to the consuls. Under the Republic, decisions of the Senate were binding. The Senate lost its independent power under the emperors.

Shrine A place where holy objects, such as statues of gods, were kept and worshipped. Most houses had their own shrines for the gods who watched over the home. Military standards were also kept in a shrine in a camp or fort.

Slave A person owned as property by another, and used as a worker. Slaves might be born from slave parents, captured in war, or bought from foreign slave dealers. People could also be sentenced to slavery for crime.

Strigil Curved metal tool used for scraping oil and dirt from the body.

Tablinum The reception room in a Roman house, where the *paterfamilias* greeted visitors and kept important documents.

Toga Large piece of cloth worn draped around the body in elaborate folds. It was the official garment of a Roman citizen.

Tribune Elected officer whose role was to protect the interests of the common people. He could veto (reject) any act of a magistrate within the city of Rome. Tribune is also the title of an army officer.

Triclinium A Roman dining room.

Triumph A victory parade, in which a general led his army through the streets of Rome, before offering sacrifices to Jupiter on the Capitoline Hill.

Villa Originally meaning a farmhouse, the word *villa* is now more usually used as the name for a large, luxurious country house owned by rich Romans. Many *villas* were centers of farming and other industries.

WHO'S WHO

Agrippina (15-59 C.E.)
Agrippina was the wife of Emperor Claudius, whom she persuaded to adopt Nero—her son from a previous marriage—as heir. She was widely believed to have poisoned Claudius, so that Nero could become emperor. Nero later had her murdered.

Augustus (ruled 27 B.C.E.-14 C.E.)
Octavian assumed the name Augustus when he became Rome's first emperor following his defeat of his rival, Mark Antony. Augustus's reign of over 40 years brought peace and prosperity to the empire after years of civil war.

Caligula (ruled 37-41 C.E.)
Rome's third emperor, Caligula was mentally unstable, demanding to be worshipped as a god. He showed such contempt for the Senate that he threatened to make his favorite horse consul. He was murdered by the Praetorian Guard after ruling for just four years.

Cicero (c.106-43 B.C.E.)
An orator, lawyer, writer, philosopher, and politician, Cicero played a leading role in the last years of the Roman Republic. He was a bitter enemy of Mark Antony, who had him killed when he took power.

Claudius (ruled 41-54 C.E.)
Emperor Claudius was proclaimed ruler after the murder of his nephew, Caligula. A popular emperor, his lasting achievement was the conquest of Britain in 43 C.E.

Cleopatra (ruled 48-30 B.C.E.)
The last Ptolemaic ruler of Egypt, Queen Cleopatra had affairs with both Julius Caesar and Mark Antony, who married her in 36 B.C.E. Following Antony's defeat at the Battle of Actium in 31 B.C.E., both she and Antony committed suicide.

Constantine (ruled 312-337 C.E.)
The first Christian emperor, Constantine ruled the west from 312 C.E., and the whole empire from 324 C.E. In 313 C.E., he granted freedom of worship to Christians. Constantine later moved the imperial capital from Rome to the new Christian city of Constantinople.

Diocletian (ruled 284-305 C.E.)
Emperor Diocletian carried out widespread reforms in the government of the empire, which he divided into two halves, each with a senior and junior ruler. Diocletian ruled the east as senior emperor.

Gaius Marius (157-86 B.C.E.)
Gaius Marius was a leading general, elected consul seven times. In 88 B.C.E., his quarrel with his rival, Sulla, over an eastern command led Sulla to march on Rome. Marius fled, but returned to seize power once Sulla was gone.

Hadrian (ruled 117-138 C.E.)
Emperor Hadrian believed that the empire had grown too big and that it needed to be strengthened. He built many frontier defenses, including Hadrian's Wall in Britain.

Hannibal (c.248-c.183 B.C.E.)
A Carthaginian general, Hannibal crossed the Alps and invaded Italy in 218 B.C.E., winning three great victories over the Roman army, including the Battle of Cannae in 216 B.C.E.

Julian the Apostate (ruled 361-363 C.E.)
Emperor Julian became known as "The Apostate" (someone who abandons his faith), because he rejected Christianity and tried to restore the worship of the old Roman gods.

Julius Caesar (c.100-44 B.C.E.)
Politician, general, and writer, Julius Caesar is famous for his conquest of Gaul, which he also described in a history, *The Gallic Wars*. In 49 B.C.E., following disputes with Pompey and the Senate, he invaded Italy and seized power. He was stabbed to death on March 15, 44 B.C.E.

Justinian (ruled 527-565 C.E.)
The Byzantine emperor Justinian reconquered many of the lost territories of the west, which had been overrun by Germanic peoples. He also had a great law code drawn up that formed the basis of many later legal systems.

Marcus Aurelius (ruled 161-180 C.E.)
A successful general, Emperor Marcus Aurelius spent much of his reign fighting to defend the empire against Germanic invaders. He was also a philosopher and author of *The Meditations*.

Mark Antony (c.82-30 B.C.E.)
One of Caesar's leading followers, Mark Antony formed an alliance with Octavian after Caesar's death. With Cleopatra, he ruled the eastern empire from 42-31 B.C.E., until he was finally defeated by Octavian.

Nero (ruled 54-68 C.E.)
One of the most notorious Roman rulers, Nero murdered his mother, stepbrother, and two wives. He loved the arts, and shocked many Romans by performing on stage. It is believed that he started the fire that destroyed much of Rome in 64 C.E.

Ovid (43 B.C.E.-c.17 C.E.)
The poet Ovid's most famous work is *Metamorphoses*. He was banished to the shore of the Black Sea in 8 C.E. His last writings describe the sorrows of exile.

Pliny the Elder (23-79 C.E.)
Pliny the Elder wrote a vast encyclopedia called *The Natural History*. He died during the eruption of Vesuvius, having gone there to conduct rescue operations.

Pompey (106-48 B.C.E.)
The general Pompey conquered large areas of the Near East in 66-63 B.C.E. He then formed an alliance with Julius Caesar, though their quarreling led to the civil war in which he was defeated in 49 B.C.E. He was murdered in Egypt.

Scipio Africanus (236-184 B.C.E.)
Scipio was the Roman hero of the Second Punic War. While Hannibal was in Italy, Scipio invaded Spain, where he captured New Carthage. He then invaded Africa, defeating Hannibal at the Battle of Zama in 202 B.C.E.

Seneca (4 B.C.E.-65 C.E.)
The philosopher, orator, and playwright Seneca was tutor to the young Nero, and a great influence on him in the first years of his reign. However, he was accused of being involved in a conspiracy against Nero, who ordered Seneca to commit suicide.

Septimius Severus (ruled 193-211 C.E.)
The general Septimius Severus seized power after a civil war. He was a ruthless emperor who, on his deathbed, told his sons to "keep on good terms with each other, be generous to the soldiers, and ignore everybody else".

Spartacus (died 71 B.C.E.)
In 73 B.C.E., the Thracian gladiator Spartacus led a revolt in the gladiatorial barracks in Capua. Although he won several battles, his rebellion was eventually crushed in 71 B.C.E.

Suetonius (c.69-c.140 C.E.)
The biographer Suetonius also served as secretary to Emperor Hadrian. His most famous work is the *Twelve Caesars*, an account of the lives of Julius Caesar and the first emperors.

Tacitus (c.55-116 C.E.)
The Roman historian Tacitus wrote two long works, *The Annals* and *The Histories*. His two short works are *Agricola*, a biography of his father-in-law who was governor of Britain, and *Germania*, on the Germanic peoples.

Tiberius (ruled 14-37 C.E.)
Rome's second emperor, Tiberius was unpopular with the people of Rome for his stinginess. Fearing assassination, he spent the last years of his reign in retirement on the island of Capri.

Trajan (ruled 98-117 C.E.)
Emperor Trajan, who was born in Spain, was an outstanding soldier and general. His campaigns led to the conquest of Dacia (Romania) and Iraq, bringing the empire to its largest size.

Vergil (70-19 B.C.E.)
The poet Vergil was the author of three works, the *Eclogues*, the *Georgics*, and the unfinished *Aeneid*, about Aeneas, the legendary Trojan ancestor of Romulus and Augustus.

INDEX

A page number in **bold** refers to the main entry for that subject.

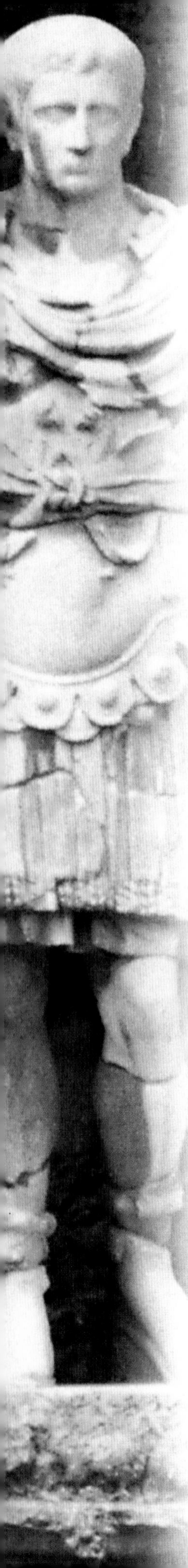

ACKNOWLEDGMENTS

Dorling Kindersley Ltd would like to thank Marion Dent for proofreading; Michael Dent for the index; Constance Novis for Americanizing; and Leah Germann and Steve Woosnam-Savage for design support. Thanks also to Conrad Mason.

Dorling Kindersley Ltd is not responsible and does not accept liability for the availability or content of any website other than its own, or for any exposure to offensive, harmful, or inaccurate material that may appear on the internet. Dorling Kindersley Ltd will have no liability for any damage or loss caused by viruses that may be downloaded as a result of looking at and browsing the websites that it recommends. Dorling Kindersley downloadable images are the sole copyright of Dorling Kindersley Ltd and may not be reproduced, stored, or transmitted in any form or by any means for any commercial or profit-related purpose without prior written permission of the copyright owner.

Picture Credits
The publisher would like to thank the following for their kind permission to reproduce their photographs:

Abbreviations key
t-top, b-bottom, r-right, l-left, c-center, ftl-far top left, tl-top left, tc-top center, tr-top right, ftr-far top right; fcla-far center left above, cla-center left above, ca-center above, cra-center right above, fcra-far center right above, fcl-far center left, cl-center left, cr-center right, fcr-far center right, fcl-far center left, cl-center left, cr-center right, fcr-far center right; fclb-far center left below, clb-center left below, cb-center below, crb-center right below, fcrb-far center right below, fbl-far bottom left, bl-bottom left, bc-bottom center, br-bottom right, fbr-far bottom right.

6 DK Images: Rough guides (cr). **7** DK Images: Rough guides (cl). **8** The Art Archive: Museo Capitolino Rome/Dagli Orti (cl); Museo Prenestino Palestrina/Dagli Orti (bl); Archeological Museum Tipasa Algeria/Dagli Orti (cr). **9** Corbis: Voz Noticias (br); Sergio Pitamitz (fbl); Jeff Rotman (bl); Photo Scala, Florence: National Museum, Belgrade (fbr). **10** akg-images: AKG (c); The Art Archive: Museo di Villa Giulia Rome/Dagli Orti (A) (ca) (fbl); Archeological Museum Florence (br); DK Images: The British Museum, London (fbr); Photo Scala, Florence: Museo Civico, Piacenza, Italy (bl). **11** akg-images: Pirozzi (t); Ancient Art & Architecture Collection: Prisma (cl); The Art Archive (br); Photo Scala, Florence (cr). **12** The Art Archive: Muzeul judetean Hunedoara Deva Romania/Dagli Orti (tl); www.bridgeman.co.uk: Musée d'Orsay, Paris, France, Giraudon (bl). **12–13** Ancient Art & Architecture Collection: C.M. Dixon (c). **13** Ancient Art & Architecture Collection: C.M. Dixon (bl); www.bridgeman.co.uk: Musée de Tesse, Le Mans, France (tl); Topfoto.co.uk: Roger Viollet (tr). **14** www.bridgeman.co.uk: Museo Acheologico Nazionale, Naples, Italy. Giraudon (t); Corbis: Araldo de Luca (bl); Werner Forman Archive (br). **14–15** The Art Archive: Musée du Louvre Paris/Dagli Orti (c). **15** akg-images: Johann Ludwig Gottfried, Historische Chronica, Frankfurt (b); Erich Lessing (t); Mary Evans Picture Library (c). **16** akg-images (bl); Erich Lessing (tl); Mary Evans Picture Library (tr); **17** The Art Archive: Dagli Orti (b); www.bridgeman.co.uk: Château de Versailles, France (t); Corbis: Gianni Dagli Orti (c). **18** akg-images: Peter Connolly (b); Ancient Art & Architecture Collection: R. Sheridan (cr). **19** www.bridgeman.co.uk: Louvre, Paris, France (bl); The British Museum, London: © The Trustees of The British Museum (ca); Corbis: Bettmann (tr); Mary Evans Picture Library (tl). **20** akg-images: Justus Göpel (bl); www.bridgeman.co.uk: Richard Westall (1765–1836) (cr); Ny Carlsberg Glyptotek, Copenhagen, Denmark (tr). **21** akg-images (cr); Vatican Museum (br); The Art Archive (tc); Galleria Nazionale Parma/Dagli Orti (A) (tl); Galleria d'Arte Moderna Rome/Dagli Orti (A) (tr); www.bridgeman.co.uk: Brooklyn Museum of Art, New York (c). **22** akg-images: Pirozzi (bl); Vatican Museum/Nimatallah (tr). **23** akg-images: (tr); Museum Kalkriese (cr); Alamy Images: Ian M Butterfield (tc); Ancient Art & Architecture Collection: Prisma (br); The Art Archive: Dagli Orti (fbl) (bc) (fbr); Jan Vinchon Numismatist, Paris/Dagli Orti (bl); DK Images: The British Museum, London (tl). **24** akg-images: Nimatallah/National Archeological Museum, Naples (bl); Ancient Art & Architecture Collection: Prisma (tr); www.bridgeman.co.uk: Musée Saint-Raymond, Toulouse, France (cl). **25** akg-images: Peter Connolly (br); Ancient Art & Architecture Collection: R. Sheridan (tr) (cra) (cr); www.bridgeman.co.uk (crb); Howard Pyle/Delaware Art Museum (tl). **26** The Art Archive: Museo della Civiltà Romana Rome/Dagli Orti (bl). **27** akg-images: Hervé Champollion (br/Castel S. Angelo); Alamy Images: Lourens Smak (crb); Ancient Art & Architecture Collection: C.M. Dixon (cl); www.bridgeman.co.uk: Musée des Beaux-Arts André Malraux, Le Havre, France/Giraudon (bl); Corbis: Vittoriano Rastelli (br/Tiber Island); DK Images: Rough Guides (tr) (cr). **28** akg-images: Peter Connolly (bl); DK Images: Rough Guides (c); Photo Scala, Florence: courtesy of the Ministerio Beni e Att. Culturali (br). **28–29** Corbis: Marco Cristofori (tc). **29** akg-images: Erich Lessing (br); Ancient Art & Architecture Collection: Prisma (tr); Photo Scala, Florence: courtesy of the Ministerio Beni e Att. Culturali (cl). **30** akg-images: (cl); Ancient Art & Architecture Collection: R. Sheridan (br); The Art Archive: Archeological Museum, Rabat/Dagli Orti (clb); DK Images: The British Museum, London (bl). **30–31** Corbis: Free Agents Limited (c). **31** akg-images: Gilles Mermet (tc); Erich Lessing/Departement des Objets d'Art, Musée du Louvre, Paris (tr); Ancient Art & Architecture Collection: R. Sheridan (tl); The Art Archive: Bibliothèque des Arts Decoratifs (bl); Museo Capitolino Rome/Dagli Orti (A) (br). **32** The Art Archive: Museo della Civiltà Romana Rome/Dagli Orti (cl) (br); Werner Forman Archive: J. Paul Getty Museum, Malibu (bc); Museo Archeologico Nazionale, Naples. (bl). **32–33** The Art Archive: Private Collection (c). **33** akg-images: Erich Lessing (bl); Eric Lessing (bc); Ancient Art & Architecture Collection: C.M. Dixon (tc); The Art Archive: Archeological Museum Madrid/Dagli Orti (br). **34** The Art Archive: Bardo Museum Tunis/Dagli Orti (fbr); Dagli Orti (br); Corbis: Alinari Archives (c); Mimmo Jodice (bl); Archivo Iconografico, S.A. (cla); Werner Forman Archive (cr). **35** akg-images: Eric Lessing (fbl); Ancient Art & Architecture Collection: A. Beecham (tr); Chris Hellier (tr); The Art Archive: Dagli Orti (bc); DK Images: The British Museum, London (bl); Utricht, The Netherlands: Wilke Schram (tl). **36** The Art Archive: Archeological Museum Naples/Dagli Orti (cr); Musée du Louvre Paris/Dagli Orti (cl); www.bridgeman.co.uk: Museo e Gallerie Nazionali di Capodimonte, Naples, Italy/Giraudon (br). **37** akg-images (tr); www.bridgeman.co.uk: Roman Museo Archeologico Nazionale, Naples, Italy (cr); Corbis: Dennis Degnan (bc); Roger Wood (tl); DK Images: The British Museum, London (cl/soot) (cl/inkpot) (clb/wax) (clb/pens); The British Museum, London (bl). **38** akg-images: Schütze/Rodemann (tc); Corbis: Arte & Immagini srl (bl); Richard T. Nowitz (bc). **38–39** akg-images: Erich Lessing (c). **39** akg-images: Vatican Museum/Nimatallah (tl); Alamy Images: Duncan Hale-Sutton (tc); Ken Welsh (ftr); Corbis: Mimmo Jodice (cr); Vanni Archive (br); Sonia Halliday Photographs (tr). **40** akg-images: Erich Lessing (br); The Art Archive: Musée du Louvre Paris/Dagli Orti (bl); DK Images: The British Museum, London (tl). **41** The Art Archive: Musée du Louvre Paris/Dagli Orti (tr); Museo Capitolino Rome/Dagli Orti (tl); Archeological Museum Cividale Friuli/Dagli Orti (bl); Photo Scala, Florence: Museo Gregoriano Profano, Vatican (br). **42** Corbis: Roger Ressmeyer (b). **42–43** The Art Archive: Dagli Orti (tc). **43** Ancient Art & Architecture Collection: R. Sheridan (clb); The Art Archive: Dagli Orti (cl); www.bridgeman.co.uk: Alinari (tr); Corbis: Jonathan Blair (crb) (bl); Mimmo Jodice (cr); Roger Wood (br). **44** akg-images: (bc); Ancient Art & Architecture Collection: R. Sheridan (bl); The Art Archive: Dagli Orti (br). **44–45** Corbis: Roger Wood (c). **45** Ancient Art & Architecture Collection: C.M. Dixon (cr); The Art Archive: Archeological Museum Naples/Dagli Orti (tr); Museo della Civiltà Romana Rome/Dagli Orti (br); Dagli Orti (cra); Antiquarium Castellamare di Stabia Italy/Dagli Orti (bl); Corbis: Mimmo Jodice (bc); DK Images: The British Museum, London (cl/bun tin) (cl/knife). **46** akg-images: Electa (tl); Sotheby's (b); Ancient Art & Architecture Collection: C.M. Dixon (cr). **47** The Art Archive: Museo della Civiltà Romana Rome/Dagli Orti (bl); Corbis: Mimmo Jodice (tr); DK Images: The British Museum, London (c) (br) (fbr); Musée du Cabinet des Médailles et des Antiques, Paris (tl). **48** akg-images (br); Erich Lessing (tl); The Art Archive: Archeological Museum Istanbul/Dagli Orti (tr); Dagli Orti (c); Museo Bottacin Padua/Dagli Orti (bl). **49** The Art Archive: Archeological Museum Naples/ Dagli Orti (tl); DK Images: The British Museum, London (tr/neclace) (tr/earrings) (tr/hairpin); The British Museum, London (cr) (bl); Roma, Musei Capitolini (br). **50** akg-images: Erich Lessing (t); www.bridgeman.co.uk: Rheinisches Landesmuseum, Trier, Germany/Giraudon (b). **50–51** Photo Scala, Florence: Courtesy Ministero Beni e Att. Culurali (c). **51** Ancient Art & Architecture Collection: R. Sheridan (cr); Michelle Williams (cb/toy horse); The Art Archive: Museo della Civiltà Romana Rome/Dagli Orti (crb); Archeological Museum Venice/Dagli Orti (c); Dagli Orti (br); Metropolitan Museum of Art New York/Album/Joseph M (tr); Museo Nazionale Terme Rome/Dagli Orti (cra); DK Images: The British Museum, London (ca) (cb/dice). **52** The Art Archive: Museo della Civiltà Romana Rome/Dagli Orti (c); Archeological Museum Venice/Dagli Orti (A) (bl); Corbis: Werner Forman (tl). **52–53** The Art Archive: Archeological Museum Beirut/Dagli Orti (c). **53** akg-images: Erich Lessing (tl) (tr); Antikensammlung, Osnabrueck, Kulturgeschichtliches Museum (crb); Ancient Art & Architecture Collection: R. Sheridan (cr); The Art Archive: Bardo Museum Tunis/Dagli Orti (tc); Archeological Museum tillon-sur-Seine/Dagli Orti (br). **54** Ancient Art & Architecture Collection: M Williams (b); The Art Archive: National Museum Damascus Syria/Dagli Orti (cr). **54–55** Ancient Art & Architecture Collection: M. Smith (t). **55** akg-images: Erich Lessing (cra); Erich Lessing (cr) (bc); The Art Archive: Museo della Civiltà Romana Rome/Dagli Orti (crb); Musée de la Civilisation Gallo-Romaine Lyons/Dagli Orti (bl); www.bridgeman.co.uk: Museo della Civiltà Romana, Rome/Giraudon (tr); Werner Forman Archive (cl). **56** Ancient Art & Architecture Collection: C.M. Dixon (cr); The Art Archive: Archeological Museum Istanbul/Dagli Orti (tl); The British Museum, London: © The Trustees of The British Museum (b); Photo Scala, Florence: courtesy of the Ministerio Beni e Att. Culturali (tr). **57** The Art Archive: Museo della Civiltà Romana Rome/Dagli Orti (tc); Art Directors & TRIP: Amer Ghazzal (cr); Photo12.com: Collection Cinema (bl); Topfoto.co.uk: The Vatican Museums/ Alinari (tr). **58** The Art Archive: Dagli Orti (r); Musée du Louvre, Paris/Dagli Orti (l). **59** akg-images (bc); Ancient Art & Architecture Collection: B. Gibbs (cr); The Art Archive: National Museum Bucharest/Dagli Orti (A) (br); National Museum Bucharest/Dagli Orti (A) (fbl) (bl) (fbr); Corbis: Araldo de Luca (tr); DK Images: Ermine Street Guard (tl/helmet) (tl/armor) (tl/cingulum) (tc/spears) (tc/knives). **60** The Art Archive: Musée du Louvre, Paris/Dagli Orti (bl). **60–61** Getty Images: Adam Woolfitt/Robert Harding World Imagery (tl). **61** Alamy Images: Skyscan Photolibrary (tr); Ancient Art & Architecture Collection: L Ellison (br); Corbis: Robert Estall (cr); Sandro Vannini (cl); DK Images: The British Museum, London (bl); The English Heritage Photo Library: Javis Gurr (fcl). **62** Alamy Images: Aerofilms (cl); Corbis: Vittoriano Rastelli (clb); Robert Estall (bl). **62–63** Corbis: James L. Amos (c). **63** akg-images: (cl) (c); Ancient Art & Architecture Collection: R. Sheridan (t); The Art Archive: Musée Romain Nyon/Dagli Orti (cr); www.bridgeman.co.uk: (b). **64** Ancient Art & Architecture Collection: R. Sheridan (l); www.bridgeman.co.uk: Museo Torlonia, Rome, Italy/Alinari (r). **65** akg-images: Rainer Hackenberg (tr); The Art Archive: Jan Vinchon Numismatist Paris/Dagli Orti (l); Topfoto.co.uk: English Heritage/HIP (br). **66–67** akg-images: Gilles Mermet (t); Ancient Art & Architecture Collection: C.M. Dixon (b). **67** akg-images: Gilles Mermet (ftr); Erich Lessing (tr); Pirozzi (cra); Ancient Art & Architecture Collection: Prisma (cb); The Art Archive: Bardo Museum Tunis/Dagli Orti (tc); Musée Luxembourgeois Arlon Belgium/Dagli Orti (clb). **68** akg-images: Nimatallah (r); DK Images: The British Museum, London (l). **69** akg-images: Erich Lessing (bl); Nimatallah (tr); The Art Archive: Archeological Museum Naples/Dagli Orti (fbl); Archeological Museum Vaison-la-Romaine/Dagli Orti (bc); DK Images: The British Museum, London (c) (br) (fbr). **70** The Art Archive: Dagli Orti (l). **70–71** The Art Archive: Museo della Civiltà Romana Rome/Dagli Orti (r); Science Photo Library: John Sanford (t). **71** akg-images: Gilles Mermet (tr); The Art Archive: British Museum, London (cla); www.bridgeman.co.uk: Museo Archeologico Nazionale, Naples, Italy (bl); DK Images: The British Museum, London (tl) (clb); Werner Forman Archive: Museo Archeologico Nazionale, Naples (cl); Jon Foster: (br). **72** akg-images: Pirozzi (br); Corbis: Gianni Dagli Orti (tl); Museum of Antiquities, University of Saskatchewan (c). **72–73** Corbis: Vanni Archive (b). **73** akg-images: Pirozzi (tc); The Art Archive: Museo Capitolino Rome/Dagli Orti (A) (tl); Staatliche Sammlung Ägyptischer Kunst Munich/Dagli Orti (tr). **74** Alamy Images: Adam Eastland (tr); Tony Lilley (bl); www.bridgeman.co.uk: British Museum, London. (l). DK Images: The British Museum, London (bc). **75** Ancient Art & Architecture Collection: R. Sheridan (tl); www.bridgeman.co.uk: Museum of Fine Arts, Houston, Texas. (tc); Corbis: Nathan Benn (b); Werner Forman Archive (cr). **76** The Art Archive: Musée de la Civilisation Gallo-Romaine Lyons/Dagli Orti (tl); Archeological Museum Naples/Dagli Orti (bl); Werner Forman Archive: Museo Nazionale Romano, Rome (cr). **77** akg-images: Erich Lessing (br); Corbis: Mimmo Jodice (t); DK Images: The British Museum, London (bl). **78** akg-images (r). Corbis: West Semitic Research/Dead Sea Scrolls Foundation (bl); Rex Features: Andre Brutmann (ABR) (cl). **79** akg-images (tl); Ancient Art & Architecture Collection: R. Sheridan (br); The Art Archive: Humor Monastery Moldavia/Dagli Orti (cr); Archeological Museum Sousse Tunisia/Dagli Orti (bl); Archeological Museum Spoleto/Dagli Orti (bc); www.bridgeman.co.uk: Bonhams, London (tr). **80** akg-images: Hervé Champollion (tr); Ancient Art & Architecture Collection: B Wilson (c); Corbis: Paul Almasy (br); Photo12.com: Oronoz (bl). **81** akg-images (br); Ancient Art & Architecture Collection: R. Sheridan (tr); www.bridgeman.co.uk (bl); Photo Scala, Florence: HIP (cra). **82** The Art Archive: Roger Cabal Collection/Dagli Orti (b); Corbis: Gianni Giansanti/Sygma (tl). **82–83** Corbis: Dave Bartruff (c). **83** The Art Archive: Musée du Louvre Paris/Dagli Orti (bl); www.bridgeman.co.uk: Dorset County Museum, UK (tr); Corbis: Archivo Iconografico, S.A. (cr) (br). **84** akg-images (tl); The Art Archive: Jan Vinchon Numismatist Paris/Dagli Orti (br). **84–85** akg-images (t); Ancient Art & Architecture Collection: C.M. Dixon (b). **85** akg-images (br). Ancient Art & Architecture Collection: R. Sheridan (tl); The Art Archive: Tesoro del Duomo Aosta/Dagli Orti (tr). **86** akg-images: Erich Lessing (tl) (cr); The Art Archive: San Vitale Ravenna Italy/Dagli Orti (A) (cl). **86–87** Corbis: Abbie Enock; Travel Ink (b). **87** akg-images (tr); The Art Archive: Biblioteca Nacional Madrid/Dagli Orti (cla); Corbis: Bettmann (tl). **88** akg-images: Robert O'Dea (bl); Alamy Images: Rex Argent (c); Britain On View (bc); Corbis: Joseph Sohm; Visions of America (tr). **89** Alamy Images: bygonetimes (br); Corbis: Dennis Marsico (bl); Getty Images: Martin Oeser/AFP (tr); Nonstock (cl).

Jacket images
Front Corbis: Bill Ross (cr); Getty Images: The Bridgeman Art Library (cl); Taxi (fcl); Rex Features (fcr). **Back** Corbis: Dennis Degnan (cr); David Sailors (fcl); Getty Images: Stone (cl); Science Photo Library: Sheila Terry (fcr). **Spine** Rex Features.

All other images © Dorling Kindersley. For further information see: **www.dkimages.com**